NAMASTEA

The Unconventional
Guide to Yoga

A.S. Salomone

*PER DIANA
GRAZIE MILLE!!*

For Matilda, Andrea, Mum 'n Dad
and my friends. Thank you for having
"tolerated" and supported me so far...
love you!

welcome to "NAMASTEA"

"The Unconventional Guide to Yoga" a parody of all things yoga. Now, before you go all namaste on me, let me make one thing clear: This ain't your typical yoga book. No, seriously, we're ditching the airy-fairy spiritual nonsense and diving head-first into the hilarity of yoga without all the fuss.

So why did I decide to write this book? Well, for pure fun. There are a whole bunch of non-believers out there who wanna get their exercise on without all that mantra-chakra-bollocks stuff. And let me tell you, finding a proper yoga course that doesn't involve soul-searching and incense burning was like trying to find a needle in a haystack.

But you know what? I was bored as f@ck and I thought: "Why not take the piss out of yoga and yogis?" And thus, this book was born—a cheeky, irreverent guide to yoga that'll have you laughing your arses off (well... at least I did it while I was writing this masterpiece!).

Inside these pages, you'll find a collection of the most unconventional and downright silly yoga practices you never knew existed. From goat yoga to disco yoga, we've got it all covered. It's yoga, but not as you know it.

So what can you do with this book? Well, you can give it as a present to your yogi-enthusiast friends for a good ol' laugh. Or you can keep it to yourself and discover that yoga is not just about bending like a pretzel and chanting like a monk. No, my friends, it's about finding joy in the daftness of life.

So grab a mat, take a deep breath, raise a glass of any booze you like, and get ready to embrace the unconventional side of yoga.

Let's have some fun, shall we?

NAMASTEA

A.S.Salomone

CONTENTS

Part 1
THE MYSTICAL 13

CHAPTER 1
Debunking the Mystical Origins: Ancient Roots and Other General Sh!t 14

CHAPTER 2
The Zen-free ZoneCiao old Mantras, welcome new Mantras . 20

CHAPTER 3
Cha Cha Chakra 29

Part 2
THE PRACTICE 49

CHAPTER 4
Yoga Anatomy made it easy! 51

CHAPTER 5
The benefits 56

CHAPTER 6
Breathe Just Like You Do When You're Not Doing Yoga! Duh! 62

CHAPTER 7
The poses 66

CHAPTER 8
Savanastashagatama The Ultimate Yoga Experience 97

CHAPTER 9
Downward-Facing Drama Queens 105

CHAPTER 10
The Great Five Warriors Unleash Your Inner Badass! 108

Part 3
THE EXTRA YOGA STUFF 111

CHAPTER 11
The Ultimate Yoga toolbox 112

CHAPTER 12
Yoga in the Digital Age 121

CHAPTER 13
Yoga Etiquette: Navigating the Do's and Don'ts with a Wink. 127

CHAPTER 14
The mythical Zen accidents, from slips n slide to Farts n burps.   131

CHAPTER 15
Yoga off mat 141

CHAPTER 16
Weird places and situations 146

CHAPTER 17
Incredibly crazy yoga classes! 155

CHAPTER 18
Into the wild 162

CHAPTER 19
Lovers   169

CHAPTER 20
Yoga Enthusiast and Their Wacky Jobs 173

WHY?
WHY NOT!

So, why the heck did I pen down this book? Well, sure, part of it was for the sheer fun of it, but the real deal boils down to a rather straightforward incident.

Picture this: My ex-partner, the mother of our adorable munch-kin, suddenly decides to embark on a yoga quest at a Buddhist centre in Brighton. And there I stood, thinking, "Why not tag along? What's the worst that could happen?."

Now, don't get me wrong, the place is renowned and a crowd-puller, but oh boy, my experience was something else entirely. The moment we stepped in, I was hit with an overwhelming sense of eerie calm. There were people with smiles glued onto their faces, a scent that would make a bloodhound question its life choices, and don't even get me started on the atmosphere. Anyway, we eventually found our way to the class, and that's when things took a turn for the ludicrous.

The guru strolled in, and the music—I kid you not—sounded like a nightmare remixed by a toddler on a sugar high (I'm more of a hardcore stuff kind of guy, mind you, electric guitars must be involved). And then came the spiel about energy, life's purpose, and other cosmic mysteries that made my brain go, "Mate, we're lost."

As if that wasn't enough, he led us into the infamous Mountain pose. You know, the one where everyone looks like they're auditioning for a "Chinese Terracotta Army's Got Talent" show. Me? Bored out of my wits, I scanned the room for an escape route. And then it happened—his eyes locked onto mine like I was an oasis of normality in a desert of mysticism. He ambled over and posed the mother of all questions: "What do you see?" My response? A real five-year-old special: "The person in front of me."

He gave me a deep, guru-like look and went all: "Gaze upon the horizon, embrace the infinite energy!" I countered with my ace card: "I'm sorry, my glasses might be dirty." Pure survival instinct, I tell ya.

Anyhow, he moved on, dismissing me like a lost cause. And that, my friends, is when I decided enough was enough. The mumbo jumbo, the pretzel poses, the Zen zones—it all started to grate on my very last nerve. So here we are, folks.

This book exists because of one man's mission to escape the clutches of mysticism and serve up some sarcasm in the face of spiritual seriousness. Absolutely, let me clarify that I'm a yoga enthusiast myself, and I genuinely love it. However, I find myself at odds with the mantras and all the mystical mumbo-jumbo that comes with it – the kind of stuff that's usually associated with meditation. In fact, I've even penned a small light-hearted e-book on the subject called "MeditHate" which you can check out on Amazon, Kobo, Applebook... or at www.medithate.my.canva.site.

Now, let's address the elephant in the room – am I a spiritual person? The answer is a resounding "No!" My faith lies in science, and that's where my comfort zone is. As I've mentioned, I engage in yoga for its physical benefits, mainly focusing on exercises and stretches. The idea behind this book is to let people in on the fact that yoga isn't just a realm of cosmic confusion; it's a practical activity involving stretching and body movements that genuinely improve one's well-being. While the tone of the book may come across as humorous and light-hearted, the message is clear: Let's take a moment to unwind, enjoy a good laugh, and remember that life's incredibly short. It's a call to relax, rejuvenate, and embrace the positives—even in the face of life's cosmic oddities!

A.S.Salomone

NamasTea

Sipping Your Way to Enlightenment, One Cuppa at a Time

Be ready for a tea-rrific revelation in the world of yoga! We've all heard of "namaste", that clichéd salutation that yogis throw around like confetti at a New Age circus. But what if I told you there's a far more superior, infinitely British way to achieve enlightenment? Say hello to the revolutionary concept of "NamasTea"!

First things first, let's dissect this namaste nonsense. It's meant to be some f@cking cosmic greeting, where you press your hands together and bow to your fellow human as if they're some enlightened being. Supposedly, it's a show of respect and unity—blah, blah, blah. But let's be honest, mate, in today's world, we could all use a more down-to-earth approach to connecting with our fellow yogis tea drinkers.

Enter NamasTea. Picture this: you're sipping your steaming cuppa, exchanging nods with your fellow tea aficionado across the room. There is no need for cosmic bowing or hand pressing. Just a subtle lift of the eyebrow that says, "Hey, I see you're on the same wavelength as me—dealing with life's nonsense one tea bag at a time."

Now, you might ask, "Why is NamasTea better?" Well, let me enlighten you, my tea-steeped friends. Unlike namaste, NamasTea doesn't require you to contort your body or give yourself a headache trying to remember if it's "na-mah-stay" or "na-mah-stay-in-bed-today." Nope, none of that. With NamasTea, all you need is a cup of your preferred brew and a good sense of camaraderie.

And let's not forget the multitude of flavours and blends that tea brings to the table. While namaste offers you little more than a slight nod and awkward silence, NamasTea opens up a world of tastes and aromas. Whether you're a fan of robust breakfast teas or delicate herbal infusions, each sip is a step toward enlightenment, minus the mystic mumbo-jumbo.

So next time you find yourself in a yoga studio, surrounded by folks mumbling namaste like they're auditioning for a role in a transcendental play, remember the superior alternative: NamasTea. Embrace the simplicity, raise your cup, and offer a knowing nod to your fellow tea lovers. It's the kind of unity that doesn't require bending like a pretzel or pretending you've achieved Nirvana on a yoga mat.

So here's to NamasTea, where enlightenment comes in the form of a warm, comforting beverage. It's time to ditch the cosmic greetings and embrace a salute that pairs perfectly with your biscuit-dunking routine. So grab your cup, raise it high, and give a nod that says, "Here's to you, my fellow tea comrade!" And remember, in the grand scheme of things, tea and unity trump pretzel poses any day of the week.

Cheers, you wise sippers of the world!

NamasTea

Note from the author: if you don't particularly like tea, feel free to substitute it with your favourite drink.

i.e.: cuppa of coffee, cuppa of beer, cuppa of water and lemon, cuppa of vodka, cuppa of Limoncello... etc etc.

Instructions
Follow the guru

Alright, you lovely lot, listen up! First things first, find yourself a cosy spot, preferably one where laughter won't send you toppling over (although a good yoga-inspired tumble can bloody well add to the entertainment!). Take a deep breath, let go of any expectations or seriousness, and brace yourself for a rollercoaster ride of comedic exploration.

Now, we understand that yoga can sometimes come with a reputation for all that seriousness and solemnity bo!!ocks. But don't you worry! In this book, we're here to turn that notion on its f@ckin' head and embrace the lighter side of yoga—I'll swear here and there just to give a lovely rude touch to it! I invite you to leave your yoga mat judgments at the door and prepare to embrace a whole new perspective—one that involves laughter, playfulness, and a willingness to embrace the absurd.

As you journey through the chapters that follow, remember that the key to fully immersing yourself in this unconventional yoga experience is to approach it with an open mind and a sense of bloody humour. Be prepared to twist and shout, both in your practice and in your laughter. Embrace the opportunity to see yoga through a comedic lens as we explore exaggerated poses, poke fun at the mystical origins, delve into the hilarious world of yoga anatomy, and more.

But we don't stop there! As you continue your feckin' trek through the pages, you'll encounter tales of yoga adventures in unexpected places, hilarious encounters with yoga influencers, and the not-so-serious side of tracking your progress through technology. You'll giggle your way through yoga-inspired language translations, explore the Zen-free zone where rock 'n' roll meets mantras, and even find yourself practising yoga in wild and unconventional settings.

I encourage you to fully immerse yourself in the experience by actively participating in the laughter yoga exercises, trying out unconventional poses, and perhaps even sharing your own funny yoga stories with friends and fellow yogis. After all, laughter is contagious, and the more we share our joy and amusement, the brighter the world becomes.

So, dear reader, we invite you to dive into this unconventional yoga adventure with enthusiasm, curiosity, and an appetite for giggles. Remember, there are no rules here, no judgments—just a joyful exploration of all the quirky and hilarious aspects of yoga. So let's embark on this journey together, one bit at a time. And who knows? By the end, you might just find yourself flexing your funny bone and embracing the unconventional in every aspect of your life. Let's laugh, learn, and share the love of yoga in its most whimsical and wondrous form!

Now, if you're bloody ready to dive head-first into this wacky world of yoga, turn the page and let the laughter begin. And don't forget, sharing is caring! Spread the joy by recommending this book to your fellow yoga enthusiasts and share a good chuckle. After all, laughter is the best way to connect, uplift, and make this world a better place. So grab your mat, put on your best smile, and get ready to embrace the unconventional with open arms.

NamasTea

PART 1
The Mystical

Chapter 1

DEBUNKING THE MYSTICAL ORIGINS: ANCIENT ROOTS AND OTHER GENERAL SH!T

Welcome, you lot of cheeky BnB*, to the land of yoga scepticism. Get ready to hop on this twisted time-traveling ride, where we'll debunk the mystical origins of yoga and other bits with a generous dose of sarcasm. So, put on your most sceptical face, and let's dive right in, shall we?

First things f@cking first, let's debunk the idea that yoga originated in some mystical realm where unicorns (yes, unicorns, because it's not yoga unless there's some mythical creature involved, right?) practiced sun salutations. Nah, my friend, yoga didn't pop out of God's arse—it was born right here on Earth, just like that dodgy casserole your aunt insists on making every bloody Christmas.

Legend has it that yoga found its roots in ancient India, where sages spent their days pulling off impossible poses and contemplating the meaning of life. But let's be real, we've all pulled off impossible poses after a few too many pints, and contemplating life's mysteries usually happens on the loo when we're in a rush for work. Picture this: a bunch of ancient sages sitting cross-legged in some dimly lit cave, contemplating the meaning of life while striking poses that would put a bloody contortionist to shame. Oh, and let's not forget the essential accessories—crystals, incense, and enough incantations to make even a Hogwarts wizard blush.

The Sanskrit word "yoga" loosely translates to "union", which sounds like some divine connection between body, mind, and soul. But let's take a moment to appreciate the irony of us modern humans striving for "union" while being glued to our bloody smartphones and barely able to have a conversation without checking Instagram. Ah, the sweet irony indeed.

Some ancient yogis claimed that yoga was a path to spiritual enlightenment, a way to transcend the limitations of the physical world. Well, that's all fine and dandy, but have you ever tried balancing in a tree pose while trying not to land flat on your face? It's more likely to lead to physical enlightenment—aka a bruised ego—than any kind of spiritual awakening.

And let's not forget about the myriad of yoga poses with names like "Lotus Pose" and "Cobra Pose." Seriously, who came up with these f@cking names? Were they having a creative block and just started tossing out random objects and animals? "Oh, look at that pretty flower! Let's call it 'Lotus Pose' because why the f@cking not?"

Alright, enough of the history lesson, my sceptical friends. The next stop on this sarcastic journey is to unleash our irreverent humour on the pretentious side of the yoga world while sipping your favourite drink (yes, you can drink during all the exercises too). So strap in, keep that eye-roll sharp, and let's poke fun at some modern-day yoga crap! But don't worry, dear BnB*, for we're here to rebrand these poses in a way that aligns with our sarcastic sensibilities. Instead of the "Lotus Pose," we'll now refer to it as the "Cross-Legged Contortionist." And the "Cobra Pose"? Well, it shall forever be known as the "Sneaky Serpent Stretch." See? Doesn't it feel more relatable already.

Let's address the whole spiritual aspect of yoga. But here's the kicker—the ancient yogis believed that practising yoga could lead to spiritual enlightenment and a higher state of consciousness. Well, I don't know about you, but my idea of enlightenment involves binge-watching Netflix with a bucket of fried chicken on my lap. But if you're anything like me, your idea of enlightenment involves binge-watching your favourite TV show while eating a tub of ice cream. Sorry, ancient yogis, but I think I'll pass on the enlightenment and go for the chocolate fudge swirl instead. Some modern yogis claim that yoga is the answer to all your problems. They'll tell you that if you just breathe deeply and stretch a little, you'll find eternal happiness, and all your bills will magically pay themselves. Well, sorry to burst their bubble, but yoga won't do your taxes or solve your relationship issues. It might make you more flexible, but it won't help you figure out how to assemble that f@cking annoying IKEA furniture without losing your sanity.

And the Mantras? Those repetitive, annoying phrases or a couple of letters that you're supposed to chant to reach a higher state of consciousness. Who came up with this sh!t? Did they just throw some random syllables together and hope for the best? "Ommmhhh" this and "Namaste" that. Frankly, we'd rather chant the menu at our favourite pizza joint. At least that way, we'd be manifesting a delicious meal. But don't you worry my lovely BnB*, I have the solution for that, where the only mantra we'll chant is "Yogalicious!"

And what about all those "energy centres" and "Chakras" that yogis claim to align and activate? Sure, we all have energy, but I'm pretty sure mine is more focused on finding the nearest coffee shop than on opening my third eye. Are they a bunch of USB ports ready to be used after a sh!t day at work? Maybe we can rename these energy centres to something more relatable, like the "Caffeine Chakra" or the "Pizza PowerPoint." I don't know about you, but my energy is more focused on finding the nearest pub than on aligning some imaginary wheels in my body.

Let's talk now about the yoga language, which sometimes sounds like it's been borrowed from a New Age dictionary. All those Sanskrit words that sound more like spells from Harry Potter on ecstasy pills than actual yoga poses "Asana," "Pranayama," "Ujjayi"... come on!

So, how about we adopt a more straightforward approach? "Pose", "Breath-work", "Deep Breathing"... that's more like it! Let's keep it simple, shall we? We'll rename classic poses with names that reflect their true essence - like the "Drunk Flamingo" for Tree

Pose, or the "I-don't-think-I-can-do-this-but-I'll-try-anyway" for Crow Pose. Stay with me because there will be special teachers to show you all!

We'll share stories of yoga mishaps that will have you in stitches, from toppling over during a balancing pose to accidentally letting out a not-so-Zen-like fart during a quiet moment of meditation (hey, it happens and there is a part dedicated to it. Farting in a yoga class it's so F@cking Zen!). So, dear reader, as we roll our eyes at yoga's ancient roots, let's remember that it's okay to embrace the practice without buying into the whole spiritual spiel. You can stretch your limbs, find balance, and even improve your flexibility without delving into the depths of your soul or summoning any ancient spirits. Just remember to breathe, relax, and keep your sense of humour intact.

Let's address the yoga attire. Some folks seem to think that you need to dress like a pretentious peacock on a gay Pride to do yoga properly. But let's be real here: you don't need a fancy designer outfit to touch your toes or do a downward dog. Sweatpants, old t-shirts, even your birthday suit, your sex-repellent PJ (I know you have one!), or naked if you're feeling adventurous—that's all you really need!

And don't even get me started on the yoga classes. There's always that one person who takes themselves way too seriously, acting like they're auditioning for the role of the yoga god or goddess. You know the type—the one with the perfectly coiffed hair and the aura of someone who's just returned from a retreat in the Himalayas. Newsflash, mate, you're not in a damn Bollywood movie! It can be stressful to be in a yoga class too. Picture this: You walk into a yoga class expecting a peaceful and serene atmosphere. But instead, you find yourself surrounded by a sea of stretchy pants, trendy mats, and more crystals than a wizard's lair. The instructor enters the room, radiating an aura of calmness that would put a sloth to shame. You wonder if this person is a yoga teacher or a walking relaxation commercial.

As the class begins, you're instructed to close your eyes and focus on your breath. Simple enough, right? Wrong! The moment you close your eyes, your mind decides it's the perfect time to remind you of all the embarrassing moments from your childhood, the grocery list you forgot to write, and that song stuck in your head that you can't stand! In an attempt to silence your racing thoughts, you take a deep breath, only to end up inhaling your neighbour's patchouli-scented aura. All your synapses are trying to survive in this tsunami of sh!t... but breeeaaath! Suddenly, achieving inner peace feels as elusive as finding matching socks in a dryer.

Oh, and let's not forget those yoga instructors who like to use the most convoluted and flowery language to describe a simple pose. "Extend your wings and soar like an eagle" for Warrior II? Come on, just tell me to spread my arms and bend my knees! Unless you won't provide me with a good magic mushroom before the class, be f@cking real! We don't need a whole novel to get into a pose, thank you very much.

Anyway, for those who claim that yoga is all about finding inner peace and letting go of material desires, well, that's all well and good. But let's be honest, we all have those moments when we catch a glimpse of ourselves in the mirror during yoga class and start wondering if our hair looks like a bird's nest or if we accidentally put our leggings on inside out. Hey, self-acceptance is all about embracing your imperfections, right?

Alright, enough of the history lesson and other sh!t, my sceptical friends. The next stop on this sarcastic journey is to unleash our irreverent humour on the pretentious side of the yoga world.

So, my eye-rollers BnB*, let's continue to laugh our way through the mystical and sometimes absurd world of yoga.

And remember always that it's okay to take yoga seriously, but it's also perfectly okay to have fun and not take it all so bloody seriously, again... Life is too damn short to be f@cking serious most of our days! Because, in the end, yoga is about finding what feels good for you and having a bit of fun along the way. So, let's continue this journey of humorous exploration, debunking myths, and embracing the unconventional in "The Unconventional Guide to Yoga".

Namaste?

A.S.Salomone

No…

NamasTea!

Note from the author:

Throughout the book, the author will address you all as BnB. It has nothing to do with Airbnb, Blizzard and Bewitched, Boozers 'n Bubbles, but Babes and Bros! Classy innit?

Chapter 2

THE ZEN-FREE ZONECIAO OLD MANTRAS, WELCOME NEW MANTRAS

Alright, listen up, you lot! Today, we're going to explore the ancient art of mumbo-jumbo – I mean, Mantras, the spiritual cheat codes. Some folks claim these magical phrases can change your life. You're telling me that if I repeat "abracadabra" enough times, I'll suddenly become a bloody wizard? Sign me up!

According to Dr. David Frawley, the Mantra guru, these things can alter your subconscious impulses, habits, and even your afflictions. Sounds like some voodoo magic, doesn't it? "Say 'Abracadabra' three times, and your beer belly will vanish!" If only life were that simple.

Oh, but wait, there's more! Chanting these Mantras is supposed to harness the power of Prana – the life force energy. It's like plugging yourself into a cosmic energy socket and hoping you'll get a power-up. I don't know about you, but I'd rather stick to my morning coffee for an energy boost, Thank you very much. And guess what, folks? Mantras can also give you a one-way ticket to spiritual states of consciousness! Move over, psychedelics – we've got a new, drug-free way to trip balls! Imagine sitting cross-legged, chanting "Hakuna Matata" and suddenly you're floating with unicorns in a cotton candy dimension. Now that's a high I'd pay to see!

Some of you might be thinking, "*But, won't these Mantras bring simplicity back into our chaotic lives?*" Oh, sure, they will! Just like wearing a snorkel in a blizzard will bring you back to the sunny beach. Simplicity, my arse! The mantra brigade will tell you to be aware of the choices you make. Well, I'm fully aware that I just ate an entire pizza by myself – and you know what? No Mantra's gonna make me feel less guilty about that! Life's already a bloody cycle of waking up, eating, working, and crashing on the couch. Now they want us to add "chanting like a deranged parrot" to the mix. No thanks!

So, there you have it, folks! Mantras – the ultimate spiritual scam of the century. If you want real change in your life, try hard work, good humour, and surely a bit of luck. As for these mystical phrases, they're about as useful as a chocolate teapot.

But hey, if you're into spiritual mumbo-jumbo, knock yourself out! Just don't expect me to join the Mantra madness anytime soon. Now, if you'll excuse me, I'm off to have a pint and a laugh – the true path to enlightenment, if you ask me! Cheers!

Enter the Mantra

Alright, you cheeky aura-w@#kers, let's dive head first into the world of yoga Mantras—the sacred chants that make us wonder if we've accidentally stumbled into a secret cult meeting. Get ready to roll your eyes and laugh your arse off at these mystical mumbo-jumbo spells.

"Om"

Seriously, what the f@ck is that all about? It's like the yogis took a nap, started snoring, and someone decided to turn it into a mantra. "Om" this and "Om" that. Are we trying to summon some ancient deity or just make weird humming noises to annoy our neighbours?

"Hare Krishna"

"Hare Krishna, hare Krishna, Krishna Krishna, hare, hare rama, hare rama, rama rama, hare hare." Oh, for the love of all that's unholy, who came up with this never-ending loop of Hare Krishna mania? How many times do we have to say this sh!t before we magically get our hands on a lifetime supply of free pizza? If only it were that f@cking easy! It's like a broken record that refuses to shut the f@ck up. We get it, Hare Krishna, you're here to haunt our dreams and infiltrate our waking hours.

Alright, you poor souls attempting to tackle these mind-bending yoga Mantras, let's have a proper laugh at these tongue-twisting chants from another dimension.

"Om namo bhagavate vasudevaya"

Seriously, what the f@ck is that even supposed to mean? It's like a magical incantation from Hogwarts that only the likes of Dumbledore can decipher. And trying to pronounce it? You might as well be attempting to speak Parseltongue after downing a bottle of Firewhisky.

"Shanti"

Is the mantra, the supposed key to inner peace. It's like trying to wish away all your problems by saying "Shanti" three times like some Mantra-abusing genie. Well, I hate to break it to you, but your inner peace ain't gonna come from chanting a word like it's some f@cking magical spell. Who the f@ck needs all that "peace" and "harmony" nonsense when we can have a glass of "Chianti" instead? Cheers to that!

"Gayatri"

It sounds like a mystical password to unlock a secret society of yoga enthusiasts. "Gayatri," are you kidding me? Sounds more like a password to a secret wine cellar filled with the finest vintages. It's the mother of all Mantras, the holy grail of enlightenment. But I gotta ask, who the f@ck comes up with these names? "Gayatri"? Is that some secret code for "Get A Yoga Teacher, Right, Immediately"? Sounds like a name for a Gay club in New Delhi.

Oh, wait for the next one...

> "Asato ma sadgamaya, tamaso ma jyotirgamaya, mrtyorma amrtam gamaya"

Seriously, are we trying to recite some ancient spell to transcend to another dimension? It's like we're auditioning for a role in a Bollywood movie without a clue what we're saying. And good luck remembering that sh!t after a few pints at the pub.

So, my fellow mantra-mumbling misfits, let's raise a glass to these cryptic chants that only the most enlightened can master. As for us, we'll stick to a simpler language that won't twist our tongues into pretzels. Cheers to keeping yoga fun and f@ckery-free!

Exit the Mantra

You might think I'm just a sarcastic bloke making fun of ancient traditions, and you'd be absolutely f@cking right! But let me tell you something, my fellow non-believers, there's a time and place for these Mantras, and it's not during a yoga class where we're all just trying not to fart in Downward Dog. So, the next time your yoga teacher starts chanting "Om" like they're auditioning for a role in a sacred choir, feel free to roll your eyes and give them a wink. And when they start with the "Hare Krishna" nonsense, join in for a laugh and see if any free pizza magically appears (btw I love pizza if you didn't notice it before).

In conclusion, my fellow sceptics, let's embrace the absurdity of these yoga Mantras and have a good laugh about them. After all, life's too short to take everything so f@cking seriously. So the next time you're at a yoga class and they bust out the chanting, remember to channel your inner sh!t and have a good old-fashioned giggle. Ciao ciao old Mantras!

NamasTea, or should I say, "F@ck it"?

Welcome new Mantras

So what do we do instead? Of course, I have the alternatives way better Mantras for you t@ssers! Here is the list of scientifically proven by me, alternative Mantras. Yes... It's a serious sh!t my friends. There are four to try and embrace the energy. Feel the Soupravanasa* energy flowing into your veins.

Enter The Mantras

"Om Shmum" – The Rock 'n' Roll Mantra

"Om" that's supposed to connect us to the frickin' universe. But let's get real, mates, sometimes it's as exciting as watching paint dry. Not anymore! We've got your back with "Om Shmum"! Picture yourself at a kickass rock concert, the crowd screaming their lungs out, and the stage set ablaze with raw energy. Now, take a deep breath and unleash a primal "Om Shmum" that roars like a goddamn rock anthem! Feel the power of electric guitars and thundering drums surge through your bones. The universe will bow down to your rock 'n' roll swagger, mate! It's like a cosmic headbang that'll make your chakras rock and roll!

INSTRUCTIONS

Step 1:   Select your favourite tune.

Step 2:   Press play on your device and put the volume up.

Step 3:   Let's get out the Mudaf@cking "OM SHMUUUUUUMMMMMM! From the top of your lungs!

Tell me... how are feeling now? Way better I'm sure!

"Hare Krishna, Hare Pizza" – The Foodie Mantra

Ah, the timeless chant of "Hare Krishna," meant to cleanse our souls and bring us closer to the divine, yeah whatever... But for some of us, the spiritual connection can be found not in the celestial realms, but rather in the deliciousness of food. So, my fellow foodies, replace the traditional "Hare Krishna" with the mouthwatering chant of "Hare Krishna, Hare Pizza!" Visualize yourself in a world where divine intervention takes the form of freshly baked pizza delivered straight to your door. Let the aroma of cheese and toppings waft through the air as you chant your way to culinary bliss. Who needs enlightenment when you can have a piping-hot slice of heaven? Let the cheesy goodness nourish your body and soul!

INSTRUCTIONS

Step 1:   Order a pizza or chuck a frozen one in the oven.

Step 2:   In the meantime, you can practice Savanastashagatama (see Chapter 7).

Step 3:   When the pizza is ready give it a bite straight away when still hot! And because the tomato sauce is f@cking hot as a volcano's lava, start the mantra "Hare Krishna, Hare Pizza, Hare, Hare, Hare, Hare, Pizza, Pizza, Muthf@cking Burning Pizza."

Step 4:   Enjoy your pizza now that cooled down.

"Namastay in Bed" – The Laziness Mantra

Alright, you lazy buggers, listen up! For those of us who'd rather stay snuggled up in our cosy beds than endure the misery of an early morning yoga session, we've got the ultimate Mantra for the lazy yogi: "Namastay in Bed!" Very clear message. Just mutter this sh!t under your breath as you reluctantly peel yourself out of your warm cocoon and offer a half-arsed salute to the universe. Embrace the power of lounging, snuggling, and hitting that bloody snooze button for the umpteenth time. Who says enlightenment can't be achieved in the comfort of your pillow fortress, right?

Screw those yoga fanatics who rise with the sun; we'll find our Zen in the land of dreams, where the only sun we want to see is the one painted on our eyelids. So, let's raise a glass, or a pint, to the noble art of laziness. In the grand tradition of lazy yogis everywhere, let us unite under the banner of "Namastay in Bed!" and proudly proclaim that our path to inner peace is paved with extra *zzzzs* and some well-deserved laziness.

So, my fellow slumber-loving slackers, let's flip the world a cheeky bird and show 'em that true serenity lies in the land of duvets and late mornings. Grab that remote, snuggle deeper under those covers, and let the world know that we're the true masters of relaxation. Cheers to the power of lounging, my fellow sloth-like souls! Now, let's get back to that sweet, sweet dreamland and tell anyone who disturbs us to bugger off!

INSTRUCTIONS

Step 1:   Prepare tea (the only activity that will consciously burn a few calories in the next 24 hours).
Step 2:   Go to bed.
Step 3:   If your brain is still lucid to trick you by telling you some activities to do, then repeat the magic Mantra: "Namastay in bed, Namastay in bed, bed bed bed".

Enjoy the peace.

"Chianti Chianti, Shandy Shandy" – The Mantra-Pub unleashed

Picture this: a yoga class where the instructor leads us in a chant of "Chianti Chianti, Shandy Shandy" instead of the usual "Shanti, Shanti, Shanti..." Oh, the bloody bliss of sipping that smooth red wine while pretending to seek enlightenment. Who needs inner peace when you can have a nice buzz going? And as if Chianti wasn't enough, let's throw in a splash of "shandy" for good measure. Who needs "illumination" when you can have a refreshing pint of shandy to quench your thirst? It's like a party on our mats, and we're all invited! Yes, my fellow yogi rebels, let's raise our f@cking glasses and toast to a yoga practice that's not afraid to have a bit of fun. Say goodbye to "Shanti" and hello to "Chianti" and "Shandy." Who needs boring Mantras when we can have a bloody good time?

A.S.Salomone

INSTRUCTIONS

Step 1:   Open a Chianti or mix a Shandy.
Step 2:   Repeat "Chianti, Chianti, Shandy Shandy."
Step 3:   Chill.

Trust me after a sh!t day at work... this Mantra is a lifesaver!

In this Zen-free Zone, we ain't got time for all that mystical mumbo-jumbo and boring Mantras. Who needs to chant like a bunch of enlightened parrots when you can unleash your inner rockstar and rebel against the yoga norms? So, let's throw away those pretentious Mantras, DO MINE instead, and grab a drink, because that's the real road to enlightenment, my friends!

Imagine, instead of "Om," we could chant "cheers" and toast to the good times. Forget "Asato ma sadgamaya," how about "let's party, muthaf@ckers!" And who needs "Hare Krishna" when we can belt out "Hell yeah, pizza!" and then be lazy and embrace the "Namastay in bed"?

It's like a yoga class meets a wild rock concert, where the only poses we care about are the ones we strike while headbanging to our favourite tunes... eat our Pizza, or be lazy and slow as a tortoise on Pregabalin! And forget about that "Shanti" stuff; the only peace we seek is when the pizza arrives and the beer keeps flowing.

In this crazy Zen-free Zone, there are no rules, no judgments, and definitely no gurus telling us how to find our inner peace. We'll find it in the guitar riffs, the laughter of our fellow yogi rebels, and the satisfaction of rocking out like there's no tomorrow or chilling all day in the name of Buddha!

In this cheeky and irreverent yoga world, we'll be chanting "Chianti, Chianti, Shandy, Shandy" while striking poses that make us feel like rockstars. No more "zen" and "serenity"; we're all about embracing the spirit of fun and laughter. So, let's bring on the Chianti and Shandy, my cheeky friends, and let the good times f@cking flow and enjoy a pizza in bed!

NamasTea with a twist of Chianti and a dash of Shandy! Cheers to a yoga practice that's as bold and f@cking edgy as we are!

*Soupravanasa

It's the primordial "soup" of energy that flows inside every human being like blood. True biology!

Note from the author: Hey there, just a quick heads up! The intention of this book is not to turn you into an alcoholic (trust me, that's not a good look). You can easily swap out alcohol for your beverage of choice (although I must admit, it won't be as hilariously wild). This is all just a light-hearted and funny read, so no need to stress. Kick back, relax, and enjoy the ride! Cheers!

Chapter 3

CHA CHA CHAKRA

Alright my dear BnB*, attention please, because we're about to delve into the mystical world of Chakras—the energy points that apparently run down your spine like a cosmic highway. But don't worry if you're scratching your head, wondering where the heck these chakras even are. You're not alone, my friends.

Chakras are the latest buzz in the "New Age" scene, and you'll hear about them more often than a pop song on repeat. Yoga class? Check. TV shows or movies with that mystical character? Double check. And of course, there's always that one know-it-all who dishes out unsolicited chakra advice like it's going out of style.

But let's face it, these chakras have a history that's as ancient and complicated as a Rubik's cube on steroids. They were first mentioned way back in the Vedas—ancient sacred texts from thousands of years ago, dating back to the time when people still thought the earth was flat.

So, what's the deal with these chakras? Well, let me give you a crash course. The word "chakra" means "wheel" in Sanskrit, which already sounds like some cosmic circus act. They say these chakras are spinning disks of energy, like a magical vortex swirling around your body. And guess what? They're supposed to stay "open" and aligned as if you're conducting some kind of energetic symphony.

Some claim there are a gazillion chakras out there—like, seriously, 114 of them. But let's keep it real, shall we? We're talking about the main ones—seven in total—that run along your spine. Like an energy highway from your sacrum to the crown of your head. Who needs the Autobahn when you've got chakras, right?

Each of these main chakras comes with its own fancy number, name, colour, and a specific area on your spine. It's like playing a mystical game of "Chakra, Chakra, Where Art Thou?" as you try to find these elusive energy hubs. But hey, they claim these chakras can impact your emotions, physical well-being, and even your coffee cravings.

So there you have it, a beginner's guide to the wacky world of chakras. Now you can join the conversation, nodding like you totally get it, even if you're still not sure how these spinning wheels of energy fit into your daily life. Just remember, my fellow truth-seekers, the chakras are out there, waiting to be discovered. So, go forth and chakra on!

But hold on to your incense sticks, because there's more to this chakra madness. Some claim you can "work" on specific chakras like they're DIY projects or something. It's like saying, "Hey, I've got a f@cking clogged chakra! Time to whip out the mystical plunger and get to work."

And don't be surprised if someone tells you they've got their chakras "aligned." It's like a metaphysical chiropractic session, but instead of adjusting your spine, they're tinkering with your cosmic energy wheels. Talk about getting a spiritual tune-up.

Now, you might wonder how the hell to keep these chakras in check. The advice ranges from yoga poses to meditation to staring at your own belly button while chanting some ancient mantra. But seriously, who has time for all that? Between work, Netflix binges, and trying to remember where you left your car keys, who's got the energy to balance their chakras like a cosmic tightrope walker?

And let's not forget the colours associated with each chakra. It's like a cosmic fashion show where your energy wheels flaunt their own personal shade. "Today, my chakra's rocking a fabulous shade of indigo, darling. What's yours?"

But in all seriousness (well, sort of), there's a lot of fascination with these chakras, and people are eager to unlock their hidden powers. They're like the metaphysical superheroes of the body, promising to cure all ailments and make you as Zen as a levitating monk.

So, if you're curious about the chakras, go ahead and dive down the rabbit hole. Just be warned, it's like exploring a mystical labyrinth where every corner holds a new surprise. But remember, whether you're a chakra enthusiast or a sceptic, it's all in good fun.

So, raise a glass (or a yoga mat) to the wacky world of chakras, where energy wheels spin, colours dazzle, and people talk about their "spiritual plumbing" like it's a normal Tuesday.

NamasTea, my fellow chakra adventurers.

May your cosmic wheels keep spinning, and hopefully you won't feel sick and puke all of your energy out!

The Cha-Cha-Chakras

Here's a list of the seven most important ones. There's no F@cking way I'm going to write about all 114 of them. Are you nut?

Root Chakra

Location: More or less up your arse
Colour: Red
Meaning: Physical identity and stability

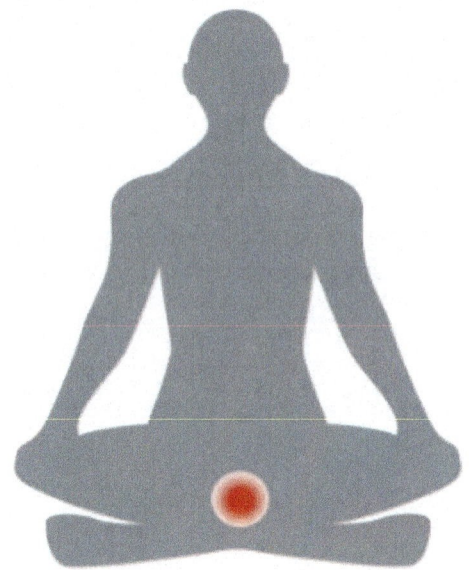

The bloomin' root chakra, snuggled right there at the bottom of your spine, like a cheeky little bugger hiding in your bum crack. 'Cause, you know, nothing screams spiritual enlightenment like having your energy centre parked in your backside, right? A blocked root chakra apparently brings a whole circus of physical issues. Forget 'bout your run-of-the-mill ailments; this bad boy delivers the real deal - arthritis, constipation, and bladder or colon problems. It's like a party in your pants, and everyone's invited, including the chakra police.

Anyway, what can I say more? It's in your arse, basically a mystical g-spot BUT be careful not to clog it! Oh no, no, no! I'm not taking any responsibility!

And don't get me started on the emotional shenanigans this cheeky chakra throws at us. What a f@cking diva! Feeling insecure about finances or our basic needs and well-being is the name of the game when this chakra decides to take a nap. It's like being on an emotional roller coaster, but instead of screams, you get a bunch of "bloody hell, what's happenin' to me?"

But don't fret, my fellow chakra fans, 'cause when this bum-dwelling energy centre decides to cooperate, we're in for a real treat. We'll feel as grounded as a sturdy oak tree, with our emotional security on par with a professional tightrope walker. It's like having a bloody emotional safety net, all thanks to this little rascal hanging out in our backsides.

So, let's raise a glass (or a cushion) to the root chakra, the ultimate champion of quirky energy centres. 'Cause nothin' says enlightenment like a chakra chillin' in your behind, am I right? Cheers to the magic of the root chakra, the arse-end of the spiritual world! And remember, folks, keep your chakras aligned.

Sacral Chakra

Location: Just below the bellybutton, just above the pubic bone. Yes right there!
Colour: Orange
Meaning: Sexuality, creativity, and pleasure

Oh, here we go again with another chakra! This time, it's the good ol' sacral chakra, and boy, does it come with some "interesting" side effects. You know it's all about pleasure, sexuality, and creativity, so get ready for a wild ride!

Picture this: You've got issues with your sacral chakra, and suddenly, your urinary tract decides to rebel like a teenage punk at a rock concert. Urinary tract infections are like the annoying gatecrashers of the chakra party, causing havoc and making you rush to the bathroom more often than a marathon runner. It's like your bladder is a moody diva, and it's taking centre stage without your permission.

But wait, there's more! Lower back pain is the surprise guest at this dysfunctional chakra gathering. It's like a relentless party crasher that never knows when to leave. It decides to camp out in your lower back, making it feel as though you've got a permanent hitch-hiker on board. And let's be honest, lower back pain is about as fun as a root canal without anaesthesia.

And if all that wasn't enough, here comes impotency, waltzing in like it owns the place. It's like a terrible stand-up comedian who just can't seem to land a joke. Your libido is on vacation, leaving you feeling as flat as a deflated balloon. It's like someone unplugged the jukebox of pleasure, and you're left with silence and awkward dance moves.

But let's not forget the emotional roller coaster that comes with this chakra mess. Your self-worth decides to play hide-and-seek like a mischievous toddler. One moment, you're feeling on top of the world, and the next, you're questioning your very existence. It's like an emotional yo-yo that never gets tired of going up and down, up and down.

Here's the kicker: this chakra is all about pleasure and creativity, but it seems to be on an extended coffee break. Your inner artist is MIA*, and your creative juices are more like dried-up raisins. It's like trying to squeeze out creativity from a rock—painful and utterly futile.

Dear friends, if your sacral chakra is acting up, just remember that it's all part of this crazy journey called life. Embrace the chaos, the awkward moments, and the wild emotional swings. And hey, if all else fails, just crack open a bottle of your favourite drink and toast to the hilarity of it all. Cheers to the sacral chakra and its wild ways!

Solar Plexus Chakra

Location: The upper abdomen, in the stomach area
Colour: Yellow
Meaning: Self-esteem and confidence

Alright, you lot, imagine if the solar plexus chakra was a bloody celebrity chef, like Gordon Ramsay on a bad day. You know it'd be serving up a culinary disaster, dishing out indigestion and heartburn like there's no tomorrow. *"This chakra is so f@cked, it makes a Michelin-starred restaurant look like a greasy spoon!"* Ramsay would scream.

And if that wasn't enough, picture this: You know it's like if the solar plexus chakra had a reality TV show. It'd be called "Gut-Wrenching Confessions," where contestants spill their guts and get grilled by their own insecurities. "Tell me, why the f@ck do you think you're worthy of love?" the chakra host would sneer.

Digestive issues. Imagine if the solar plexus chakra was a prankster with a twisted sense of humour. You know, it's like if it decided to play "Chakra Bingo" with your digestive system: *"Oh, today's special is heartburn and constipation! Congrats, you won the sh!tty prize!"* it'd laugh in its sadistic chakra voice.

And what about self-esteem and self-confidence? Imagine if the solar plexus chakra was a stand-up comedian, delivering punchlines that hit you right in the gut. *"Why did the chicken cross the road? To escape your crippling self-doubt!"* it'd joke, leaving you in stitches of both laughter and existential crisis.

But hey, amidst the chaos and the comedy, there's a lesson to be learned. You know it's like if the solar plexus chakra was a quirky life coach, pushing you to embrace your imperfections and laugh at your struggles. *"Darling, you're a hot mess, and that's bloody brilliant!"* it'd say, giving you a cheeky wink.

So, my friends, let's raise a glass (again of course) to the solar plexus chakra, the twisted chef, the ruthless reality TV host, the prankster, and the stand-up comic all rolled into one. Embrace the absurdity, laugh at the madness, and remember, we're all just trying to navigate this gut-wrenching journey of self-discovery. Cheers to the solar plexus chakra, the f@cked-up fountain of indigestion and self-awareness! Now go forth and tackle life with a pinch of humour and a dash of chakra enlightenment.

NamasTea

Heart Chakra

Location: Duh!
Colour: Green
Meaning: Compassion and love

Almost done dear BnB*, this chakra is the one that loves to play tricks on us and mess with our emotions. Brace yourselves for some heart-wrenching revelations about this middle-of-the-road chakra that loves to meddle in our lives.

Picture this: Your heart chakra decides to go on strike, and suddenly, you're having more heart problems than a marathon runner with a love for gigantic doughnuts. It's like your heart is on a roller coaster of emotions, going up and down faster than a kid in a candy store. You've got heart palpitations like a drummer on speed, and it feels like your chest is staging a full-blown revolt.

And let's not forget about the asthma that comes barging in like an uninvited guest. It's like trying to breathe through a straw while running fast like a cheetah. You're gasping for air like a fish out of water, and it feels like your lungs are hosting a never-ending yoga class for stress.

Oh, and how about those weight issues that love to crash the heart chakra party? It's like your metabolism has decided to play hide-and-seek, leaving you feeling like you've got the world's slowest metabolism. It's like your body is a rebellious teenager, refusing to cooperate and making you feel like you've got a permanent food baby.

But the real fun begins with people's actions when their heart chakra is blocked. They turn into self-sacrificing saints, putting others first to their own detriment. It's like they're auditioning for the role of a martyr in a Shakespearean tragedy. They've mastered the art of neglecting their own needs in the name of love, and it's like they're on a one-way ticket to emotional burnout.

Basically, this chakra is the bridge between our upper and lower chakras, a real emotional tightrope act. It's like balancing on a unicycle while juggling chainsaws. One wrong move, and you're spiralling into a pit of loneliness, insecurity, and isolation. It's like being stuck on an emotional roller-coaster ride that never seems to end. Sweet innit?

But hey, don't let the f@cking heart chakra drama get you down. Embrace the chaos, the heart flutters, and the emotional turmoil. Remember, you're not alone in this crazy journey, and we're all just trying to figure it out one chakra at a time. So, cheers to the heart chakra and its wild, unpredictable ways. Here's to embracing the roller-coaster ride of emotions with a toast to life's hilarity!

Throat chakra

Location: Guess…
Colour: Blue
Meaning: Communication

The notorious throat chakra, the talkative troublemaker of the bunch. Get ready for some verbal shenanigans as we dive into the world of throat chakra drama.

So, imagine this: You wake up one day with a sore throat that feels like you've swallowed a cactus. It's like your vocal cords are staging a protest, refusing to cooperate, and leaving you sounding like a frog with a hangover. Also (of course) on the teeth and gums that decide to join the party. It's like a dental disaster zone in there, with more drama than a soap opera.

But wait, there's more! When the throat chakra goes haywire, you become a master of dominating conversations. It's like you're the one-man show, and everyone else is just there for the ride. You talk so much, people start wondering if you've been hired as the spokesperson for a chatty charity.

And let's not forget about the gossiping that creeps in like a nosy neighbour. It's like you've become the town's official gossip guru, dishing out juicy tidbits like a tabloid columnist. But hey, who needs privacy when you can be the life of the gossip party, right?

Oh, and speaking without thinking? Well, that's your new superpower. It's like your brain has gone on vacation, leaving your mouth in charge of the verbal chaos. You blurt out things that would make a sailor blush, and it's like you've become a walking, talking, uncensored comedy show.

Perhaps the most f@cking annoying part is having trouble speaking your mind. It's like your thoughts are playing hide-and-seek, and you can't seem to find the right words when you need them the most. It's like trying to solve a Rubik's Cube blindfolded while riding a unicycle (I guess some people can).

But fear not, my chatty comrades! Embrace the throat chakra roller coaster and its wild verbal adventures. Remember, it's all part of the hilarious journey of self-discovery. So, let's raise a glass (as usual) to the throat chakra and its mischievous ways. Here's to speaking your mind, listening with compassion, and knowing that sometimes, it's okay to unleash verbal madness and let the words flow freely.

Third eye chakra

Location: Between the eyes, on the forehead, which is why it's also known as the "brow chakra"
Colour: Indigo
Meaning: Intuition, Imagination

Third eye chakra, the mystical eye in the middle of your forehead! Really? You know it's like if it thinks it's some sort of all-knowing guru, but really, it's just a glorified optometrist with a superiority complex. "*I see all, I know all!*" the chakra would boast, but let's be honest, it probably needs a good pair of glasses to see beyond its own delusions.

And let's talk about those headaches and hearing problems. Imagine if the third eye chakra was a drama queen (more or less like the ones) with a flair for theatrics. You know it's like if it threw daily tantrums, causing migraine mayhem and making you hear voices that sound like they're straight out of a bad soap opera.

"*Oh, woe is me, I'm so enlightened, and yet I can't handle a little pressure in my head!*" the chakra would moan.

When it comes to intuition, imagine if the third eye chakra was a fortune teller at a dodgy fairground. You know it's like if it claimed to see the future, but all it really did was make vague and unhelpful predictions. "*I sense that something might happen, or maybe it won't, who knows?*" it'd say with a mysterious wink, leaving you more confused than ever.

And what about those people who think they "know it all" because their third eye chakra is supposedly open? Imagine if the third eye chakra was a smug know-it-all at a pretentious cocktail party. You know it's like if it looked down its nose at everyone else, pretending to have all the answers while secretly being clueless about life. "*Oh, darling, you're so lost, let me enlighten you!*" the chakra would condescend.

But hey, amidst the absurdity and the antics, there's a glimmer of truth. You know it's as if the third eye chakra was a quirky life coach, urging you to trust your instincts and see beyond the surface. "*Listen, my friend, forget the theatrics, tap into your inner wisdom, and see the bigger picture!*" it'd advise, giving you a wink of genuine insight.

So, my fellow seekers of enlightenment, let's raise a bottle (for change) to the third eye chakra, the diva optometrist, the drama queen fortune teller, the smug know-it-all, and the quirky life coach all wrapped up in one. Embrace the chaos, laugh at the mystical drama, and remember, true insight comes from within. Cheers to the third eye chakra, the hilarious hub of headaches and half-baked prophecies! Now go forth, my wise yet wonderfully clueless souls, and see the world with both your eyes open.

And finally...

The Crown chakra

Location: Top of the head
Colour: Purple or White
Meaning: Awareness and intelligent

Ah, the crown chakra, the big boss of the chakra gang. Get ready for some cosmic comedy as we explore the crown chakra's reign over the rest of the chakra crew.

The crown chakra is like the puppet master, pulling all the strings and controlling every organ in the chakra system. It's like a chakra dictatorship, where the brain and nervous system are at its beck and call. All the other chakras bow down to its authority, like a bunch of chakra minions.

But beware, for a blocked crown chakra can turn you into a narrow-minded, sceptical, and stubborn know-it-all. It's like you've swallowed the "I know everything" pill and refuse to see beyond your own limited perspective. You become the grandmaster of scepticism, questioning everything and believing nothing unless it's written in the stars; and when this chakra is open, get ready for the cosmic show!

It's like a flood of bliss and enlightenment washes over you, leaving you feeling like the Dalai Lama on a roller-coaster. You're floating on a cloud of spiritual euphoria, and it's like you've unlocked the secrets of the universe over a cup of tea.

But hey, who needs to see the bigger picture when you've got the crown chakra calling the shots? You're on top of the world, and nothing can bring you down from your chakra throne. You're the enlightened emperor, ruling over your own little chakra kingdom.

So, embrace the crown chakra's cosmic antics and let it take you on a wild ride through the realms of enlightenment. But remember, even the crown chakra needs a reality check now and then. It's like a chakra rock star going on tour—keep the other chakras in harmony, and you'll be the crown chakra's number-one fan.

Now go forth, my spiritually sadistic friend, and let the crown chakra's cosmic comedy be your f@cked up guiding light!

And there you have it, my fellow chakra explorers! The cosmic world of chakras is a hilarious mix of feelings, energy, and enough drama to rival a f@cking soap opera. But don't take it too seriously, 'cause, at the end of the day, we're all just a bunch of clueless humans trying to figure out this cosmic puzzle.

So, the next time someone starts preaching about chakras, just nod and smile while secretly thinking, "*Yeah, right, like I know what the f@ck you're talking about!*" Because let's face it, chakras may be the buzzword of the moment, but who the hell knows if they're the real deal or just some ancient hocus pocus?

But yo, whether you're a die-hard chakra believer or a sceptic with a side-eye, one thing's for sure: this journey through the chakras has been a f@cking trip! From the root to the crown, we've explored every nook and cranny of our energetic centres, and let's not forget the hilarious detours along the way.

So, my fellow chakra comrades, let's raise a toast to this absurd adventure of self-discovery! May your chakras be as balanced as a tightrope walker on a unicycle, and may you find bliss and enlightenment amidst the chaos of life.

And if anyone ever tries to convince you that their chakras are more enlightened than yours, just tell them to go take a f@cking hike! Because at the end of the day, we're all on this crazy journey together, stumbling, laughing, and occasionally face-planting into the unknown.

The Cha Cha Chakra Family!

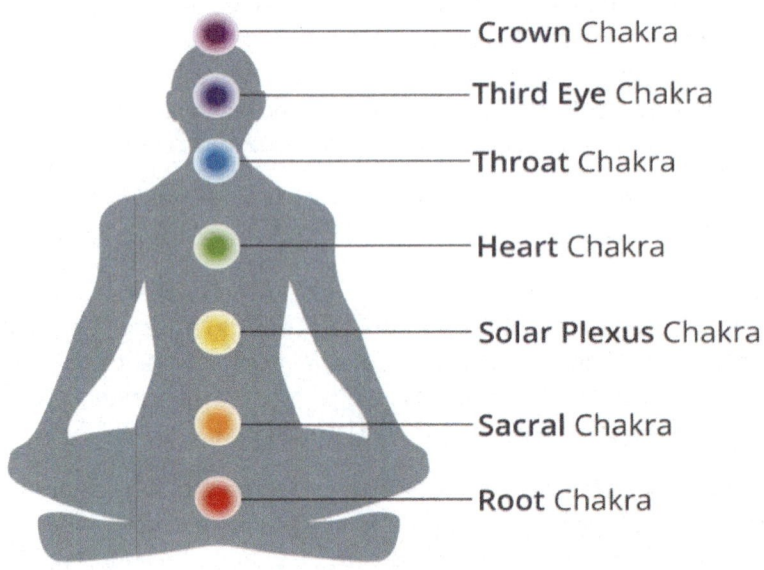

So, cheers to the Chakras, the ultimate cosmic comedy show, where emotions run wild, energy spins out of control, and the punchline is always just a f@cking surprise away. Embrace the laughter, relish the chaos, and never forget to sprinkle a healthy dose of scepticism on top of this chakra fiasco. And with that, my dear chakra warriors, it's time to bid adieu to this roller-coaster of feelings. Until next time, keep laughing, keep exploring, and never stop questioning the mystical mysteries of life. And remember, when in doubt, just blame it on the chakras!

NamasTea Chakratists!

PART 2
THE PRACTICE

NamasTea

Introduction to the "Real" yoga, the serious sh!t

Hello yoga rookies and flexible fanatics, welcome to the bloody circus tent called "The Practice." Now, if you thought Part 1 was a wild ride through the realm of yoga fluff, hold on to your Lululemon leggings, 'cause we're about to dive into the kale-smoothie-fuelled madness of contorted enlightenment. And if you ain't already clutchin' your chakras like they're last call at the pub, well, you're in for a treat.

In this round of the yogi rodeo, we're wrangling with poses that'd make a gymnast cry for mercy and a rubber band disown its stretchy heritage… naaa we chill! Don't you worry! I mean, who needs to do the hokey-pokey when you can twist and turn a bit. In the sea of serene faces – the yogis – who're so Zen, they make a sloth on a hammock look like a caffeine-addled squirrel on Red Bull, you will see few poses to give you an idea how to stretch easily.

But lads and lasses: while we might be mockin' and takin' the mick, there's a certain absurd beauty to this whole yoga charade. It's like watchin' a bunch of grown adults pretend they're noodles with delusions of nirvana. So, strap in – or maybe strap on, if that's your thing – 'cause we're delvin' into the heart of The Practice, where you'll find more bends, twists, and ego-flexing than a reality TV show audition.

So, roll out your mats, flex them fingers, and prepare to stretch your sense of reality as we navigate through the whimsical wonderland of yoga's greatest hits; and most important:

DO NOT OVER DO IT!

NamasTea, you cheeky BnB – let the bending begin.

Chapter 4

YOGA ANATOMY MADE IT EASY!

Alright, brace yourself for a no-holds-barred journey into the freakin' absurd world of yoga anatomy. Strap on your f@cking lab coats, because we're gonna get all scientific and sh!t.

So, yoga anatomy, huh? It's like learning the f@cking blueprints of your own body so you can twist yourself into a human pretzel without breaking any bones. Who needs a guru when you can be your own anatomical f@cking engineer? Anatomy, physiology, blah blah blah. It's all about knowing which part of your body is responsible for making you feel like a superhero when you nail that goddamn crow pose, and which part of your body is screaming at you to just lie the f@ck down and order a pizza instead.

Listen up, my friends, you don't need to be a bloody brain surgeon to understand this sh!t. Just read some articles, watch some videos, and for f@ck's sake, use that thing called a brain to absorb the info.

But let's get real here. Yoga anatomy is a bottomless pit of knowledge. You could spend a lifetime trying to figure it all out, and you'd still feel like a f@cking yoga freshman.

Alright, alright, let's get more real than a reality TV show, shall we? I'm not here to sugar-coat sh!t or blow smoke up your downward-facing ass. So, here's the f@cking truth about yoga anatomy: it's a maze of twists, turns, and mind-boggling jargon.

But guess what? You don't need a Ph.D. in f@cking anatomy to survive the yoga jungle. Here's the simple secret: LISTEN TO YOUR BODY! Yeah, that's right. When you stretch, your body's gonna talk to you louder than your nagging mother-in-law.

Now… shall we make it easy for everyone?

When do you start feeling like your ligaments are about to go on strike? F@ck that stretch! Ease up, take a breath, and work your way into it progressively. Your body ain't no rubber band, and you sure as hell don't want to end up in a yoga disaster viral video.

And let's talk about those show-off gurus who twist themselves into pretzels while balancing on a damn toothpick. Don't be fooled, my fellow yogis. Some of them are either Photoshopped with AI technology, or they are as skinny as a Biafra kid. Seriously, they probably eat air and dreams for breakfast, they might not have 10 pounds of extra fat wrongly distributed in their belly… so chill out again and don't stress your bones, muscles and ligaments in these "Kamasutra of self-sex pleasure" contortions extreme yoga poses. Especially if you're just starting out, don't even think about attempting those circus-like positions. Unless you've been doing yoga since the day you were born, your body ain't ready for that sh!t. So, don't go contorting yourself into an invertebrate just yet, 'cause you'll end up in the ER faster than you can say "OM." ("OMmy God, I think I f@cked up my hamstrings"… then you can use the Mantra OM).

So, here's the golden rule of yoga anatomy: stretch, bend, and twist at your own f@cking pace. Take it easy, my friends. Rome wasn't built in a day, and neither will your perfect yoga pose. Embrace the journey, laugh at your f@ck-ups, and remember, it's all about the progress, not the perfect pose.

But don't worry my fellow BnB* yogis, as you don't need to be a Ph.D. in f@cking anatomy to rock your yoga practice. All you need is a bit of curiosity, a pinch of interest, and a whole lot of f@cking good determination. You'll be bending and twisting like a pro in no time, even if you still can't pronounce half the f@cking bones in your body.

Alright, listen up, my fellow curious friends! If you're craving some brainy stuff on the anatomy of yoga, you can dive into the never-ending abyss of internet info. But let's be real here—most of that sh!t is as boring as watching two sloths playing chess, and this book ain't here to lull you into a coma.

BUT, don't worry! Your friendly neighbourhood yoga renegade (that's me, by the way) has got some scientifically proven gems to share. I mean, I spent a whopping 35 minutes doing intense research while battling myself in a rousing game of Jenga (because why not?).

So, buckle up, my brainy rebels, and get ready for the ultimate yoga anatomy knowledge. The stuff they won't teach you in those dusty textbooks. Are you ready? Let's go!

The Fecking Elastic Ligaments

Oh, yes, those stretchy bands that hold our bodies together are like the daredevils of the human anatomy. They're like, "Hey, you wanna stretch me? Sure, go ahead! But don't blame me when I snap back like a rubber band on steroids!" So, when you're contorting yourself like a yoga pretzel, listen up! Your ligaments are the real acrobats, and they'll let you know when you're pushing it too damn far. So, chill the f@ck out and respect the bounce, okay?

Bones That Love a Good Chill

We all have those show-off yogis who twist and bend like they've got a backstage pass to Cirque Du Soleil. But hold on a second! As I said previously, either they've got a secret Photoshop trick on the side, or they're blessed with being 10 pounds lighter and skinnier than you. Or, better yet, they've been doing yoga since the age of dinosaurs. So, don't let their crazy moves convince you to break your bones trying to keep up with the contortion Olympics.

The Mysterious Nervous System

Ah, the mysterious realm of nerves and their message-transmitting ways. It's like a secret yoga spy network inside your body. But hey, you don't need to be a top-notch scientist to know that the nerves in your spine won't summon the universe for you. So, chill, take a deep breath, and let the spies do their thing.

Yoga Master or Sorcerer?

There's always that one yogi who seems to defy gravity and levitate during meditation. You can't help but wonder if they're a yoga master or secretly wielding a broomstick under their yoga pants. Either way, they've got us all bamboozled. But who gives damn a sh!t? I'm just an office rat, bent on a laptop for nine hours a day and I need to prevent it to be broken at the age of fifty, that's all!

Alright, gather 'round, you lot of yoga enthusiasts – or should I say, potential mad contortionists ? Now, I'm no yoga whisperer, but if you're thinking of launching yourself into a twisty pose without giving your muscles a bit of a heads-up, you're as clever as a penguin in the Sahara. Imagine this: you're attempting to coil up like a spring while your muscles are still in their pyjamas, sipping their morning tea. It's like asking a snail to participate in a drag race without a turbo boost.

Let me paint you a picture of the utter chaos that unfolds when you ditch the warm-up and dive straight into the yoga deep end. It's akin to asking a goldfish to perform Hamlet – a tragicomic disaster waiting to unfold. It's as though you're trying to balance on a tightrope while juggling flaming torches and reciting the periodic table backwards – a recipe for a slapstick calamity. Remember that bloke who believed he could contort into a human pretzel after a full English breakfast? Well, he ended up more knotted than a phone charger in a teenager's backpack.

If you're keen on dodging the injury bug, do yourself a favour and treat your muscles to a polite chat before you subject them to your yoga whims. I mean, you wouldn't take a greyhound for a sprint without letting it stretch its legs, would you? It's common courtesy, like offering your muscles a biscuit before their grand performance.

So, the next time you're pondering a downward dog or an upward drunk flamingo – or whatever whimsical creature pose tickles your fancy – remember to give your muscles a heads-up, or you'll end up stiffer than a royal's upper lip at a commoner's joke.

My fellow rebels of the yoga realm, keep your minds open, your curiosity alive, and don't take this sh!t too seriously. After all, yoga's about finding the fun and laughing at the absurdity of it all.

NamasTea, you daring explorers of yoga's mysterious underbelly!

Chapter 5

THE BENEFITS

Alright, listen up, you bunch of yoga-curious muppets, let's cut through the airy-fairy fluff and get to the sweaty heart of the matter – the real benefits of this bendy bonanza. Forget about floating on clouds and aligning your bloody chakras; we're talking about getting down and dirty with those poses that'll have you sweating like a sinner in church.

First off, let's address the elephant in the room – flexibility. I ain't talking about some spiritual journey to meet your inner unicorn; I'm talking about stretching those limbs like a bloke trying to fit into last year's skinny jeans after a Christmas feast. You'll be twisting and turning like a contortionist in a circus, but without the freaky costumes and applause. Remember that time you tried to touch your toes and felt like a rusty robot? Well, wave goodbye to that nonsense. Yoga's like WD-40 for your body – it'll have you moving and grooving like a limber circus performer. Imagine reaching for the remote without pulling a muscle – sounds like a win, right?

Here, are 17 benefits from Yoga that you will have if you put a bit of effort into it:

1 Strength - I ain't spouting some namby-pamby "strength of the soul" nonsense. I'm talking about muscles so tight you'll give the Incredible Hulk a run for his steroids. Those fancy poses might look like a cross between interpretive dance and a human knot, but they're sculpting muscles that'll have you flexing like a gym junkie on a selfie spree. No need to pump iron like a muscle-bound gym rat. Yoga's sneaky like a ninja, working on muscles you didn't even know you had. Those weird and wonderful poses? They're like a secret superhero training for your whole body. Who needs to lift weights when you can do a "downward dog" and be your own Iron Man?

2 Balance - not the sort that involves harmonizing your chakras or aligning your bloody aura. I mean, standing on one leg without wobbling like a piss-drunk sailor on a dodgy ship. While those enlightened souls are off meditating with incense and OM-chantin', you'll be standing tall, teetering on one foot like a flamingo with a purpose. You might not be walking a tightrope anytime soon, but that doesn't mean you can't have balance like a circus star. Yoga's all about standing on one leg, pretending you're a tree – talk about multitasking, eh? Before you know it, you'll be strutting around like a flamingo with a swagger.

3 Stress - And let's not forget the ultimate stress-buster – no sage smudging or candle-lit ceremonies required. The sweat you'll be dripping during these workouts is like a detox for your worries. Picture this: you're sweating out your job stress, relationship drama, and daily grind like a bloody warrior fighting for their sanity. Stress is like that annoying friend who won't leave you alone. Enter yoga – the ultimate body-and-mind tranquilliser. Think about: you're stretching and posing away your worries like you're sweeping 'em under a cosmic rug. By the end of it, you'll be so chill, you might as well have melted into a puddle of calm.

4 Mood - Ever seen someone frowning in a yoga class? Nah, didn't think so. Yoga's like a happiness factory, pumping out those good vibes like there's no tomorrow. Whether it's the exercise, the deep breaths, or just the fact that you managed not to trip over your own feet, your mood's bound to get a makeover.

5 Mind - Yoga isn't just about twisty poses; it's a brain workout too. Ever tried concentrating while balancing on one foot? It's like solving a puzzle, but with the added bonus of not fallin' flat on your face. Plus, all that breathing and focus helps you tune out the noise and find your Zen – even if it's just for a few blissful moments.

6 Pain Relief Buddy - Ready to show those pesky aches and pains the exit door? Yoga's your new BFF in this battle against discomfort.

Imagine those grumpy joints and tense muscles throwing in the towel as yoga's gentle stretches and poses work their charm. Wave ta-ta to that cranky lower back that's been acting like a party pooper – yoga's here to throw it the ultimate shindig. So whether it's a neck that feels more stubborn than a mule or shoulders that have been acting diva-like, yoga's your backstage pass to a pain-free life. Time to roll out the mat and give those aches a run for their money – they won't know what hit 'em!

7 Immune System Defender - Yoga's not just striking a pose – it's gearing up to be your immune system's ultimate superhero. Say adios to those annoying bugs and sniffles, because yoga's here to arm your body's defences. No more surrendering to every cold and flu that crosses your path – with yoga on your side, you'll be giving those pesky invaders a run for their money. So, while you're striking your best warrior pose, just remember that your immune system's right there with you, ready to tackle whatever the world throws your way. NamasTea, bugs – yoga's got this!

8 Anxiety Vanquisher - Ready to give those racing thoughts a run for their money? Yoga's your secret weapon in the battle against mind-boggling anxiety. Say 'cheerio' to those worry marathons, because yoga's here to kick 'em to the curb. It's like giving anxiety a one-way ticket to the Bermuda Triangle – 'cause once yoga steps in, there's no turning back. So, while you're busy twisting and bending on the mat, just know that your mind's getting its much-needed chill pill. Keep calm and yoga on, 'cause anxiety's got nothing on you!

9 Breath Revolution - Ready to unleash the lung power of a dragon? Yoga's your breath coach, showing those lungs who's boss. It's like a deep-sea diving lesson for your respiratory system – you'll be inhaling and exhaling like a serene sea creature. No more shallow huffs and puffs – yoga's here to give your body an oxygen infusion that'll make you feel more alive than ever. So, as you strike those poses and flow through sequences, just know that your lungs are gettin' a VIP ticket to a world of better breathing. Breathe easy, my friend – yoga's got you covered!"

10 Heart's Best Friend - Got a soft spot for that ticker of yours? Well, guess what – yoga's feeling the love too! It's like a heart-to-heart chat with your cardiovascular system, giving it a boost like a high-energy smoothie. Say 'bye-bye' to high blood pressure woes, because yoga's got the magic touch that'll keep your heart humming in tip-top shape. So, while you're stretching and flowing on the mat, just remember that your heart's in for a wellness treat that'll have it ticking with happiness. Love your heart, and let yoga show it some major love back!

11 Posture Prodigy - Ready to give that slouch the boot? Yoga's your posture boot-camp, turning you into a stand-tall sensation that'll put skyscrapers to shame. Say sayonara to the hunch, because yoga's in the business of making you strut like a confident peacock. No more feeling like a wilted flower – yoga's here to straighten you out, quite literally. So, as you strike those poses and find your balance, just remember that you're training to be the next posture superstar. Stand tall, my friend – you've got yoga as your back-ally!

12 Fat-Burning Sidekick - Ready to put those calories on a bonfire and send fat packing? Yoga's your trusty partner in the quest for your happy weight. It's like having a metabolism-boosting dance party right on your mat. Say 'adios' to those extra pounds, because yoga's got your back in the battle against excess baggage. So, as you flow through poses and get your sweat on, just remember that you're on a weight-loss adventure with yoga as your fearless guide. Torch those calories, my friend – and let yoga be your ultimate slim-down sidekick!

13 Dreamland Conductor - Ready to banish those late-night staring contests with the ceiling? Yoga's your lullaby for kicking insomnia to the curb and embracing sweet, sweet dreams. It's like a bedtime story that guides you into a land of restful slumber. Say 'nighty-night' to tossing and turning, because yoga's here to tuck you in and whisk you away to the world of peaceful sleep. So, as you wind down and settle into those relaxing poses, just know that you're on a journey to becoming a sleep champion with yoga as your sleepy-time conductor. Sweet dreams, my friend – yoga's singing you a lullaby to the land of Zzzs!

14 Digestion Dynamo - Ready to give your belly a happy dance? Yoga's like a gentle massage for your insides, making sure your digestion flows smoother than a well-polished river stone. Say 'adios' to belly bloat and digestive troubles, because yoga's got the moves that'll keep things moving. So, as you twist and stretch like a pretzel, just remember that your tummy's getting a soothing rubdown from yoga's expert hands. Keep those internal gears greased and ready to roll, my friend – yoga's your digestion's best friend!

15 Energy Escalator - Ready to give your energy levels a lift without the dreaded crash? Yoga's your caffeine-free pick-me-up that'll have you feeling refreshed and revitalized. It's like a shot of espresso for your body and mind, minus the jitters. Say 'goodbye' to that midday slump, because yoga's here to be your natural energy elevator. So, as you flow through poses and recharge your batteries, just remember that you're on a journey to feeling more awake and alive than ever. Energize, my friend – and let yoga be your ultimate pep talk!

16 Body Whisperer - Ready to decode the mysteries of your own body? Yoga's like a secret language lesson, helping you tune into your body's signals and desires. It's like becoming a detective of your own well-being, solving the puzzle of what your body really wants. Say 'so long' to ignoring those niggles and cravings, because yoga's here to be your body awareness ninja. So, as you flow and move mindfully, just remember that you're on a quest to become a true master of understanding what makes your body tick. Listen, learn, and unlock the secrets of feeling your best – yoga's your guide!

17 Youthful Wizardry - Ready to give Father Time a run for his money? Yoga's your very own fountain of youth, keeping you feeling and looking spry without needing a time machine. It's like a magical potion that slows down the clock and keeps your energy levels up. Say 'adios' to feeling like a relic, because yoga's here to work its age-defying wonders. So, as you flow through poses and embrace your inner Peter Pan, just remember that you're on a journey to keeping that youthful sparkle alive. Stay vibrant, my friend – yoga's your timeless spell for feeling forever young!

So there you have it, folks – the nitty-gritty of why yoga's like a magical potion for your body and soul. Flexibility, strength, balance, stress-busting', mood-boosting, and brain-training — all rolled into one quirky, twisty, and downright fun package. Roll out that mat and get ready to strike a pose, 'cause whether you're a yoga newbie or a seasoned pro, this journey's gonna have you feeling like the rock star of your own wellness show. Namaste, you yoga warriors — let's get stretching!

I'm absolutely flabbergasted by my charming, dear BnB! Would you believe it – not a single expletive slipped out of my fingers while penning this chapter! Sweet mother of surprises! I might need a stiff drink to fathom this remarkable feat. It's like a magic trick that defies all odds. So, here's to a round of celebratory beverages — a toast to this unexpected, curse-free accomplishment that's left me both amused and thirsty.

Cheers, my friends!

Chapter 6

BREATHE JUST LIKE YOU DO WHEN YOU'RE NOT DOING YOGA! DUH!

Ciao bendy, stretchy, wannabe-contortionists! Today's topic is the "pièce de résistance" of yoga: breathing. And let me tell ya, it's a real game-changer, but not in the mystical, cosmic, "let's float away on a cloud of chakra-fuelled unicorn farts" kind of way. Nah, we're gonna break down this breathing nonsense into what it actually does for your bodily sack of skin and bones.

So, let's imagine you're just chilling', stuffing your face with a bacon sandwich or sippin' on a pint of the good stuff, yeah? Well, guess what? You're breathing! Astonishing, innit? You're sucking in oxygen, that good ol' air-stuff that keeps your organs from throwing in the towel. And when you're doing your yoga, you're still breathing—well, unless you're a complete bloody idiot and forgot how to do that... really? Not even if you have a single f@cking neuron suffering from a panic attack, left in that useless sponge that Mother Nature mistakenly placed in your skull, which, by the way, seems to have more useful purposes when it's empty! I have to say, in this world we are living in, we are surrounded by fucking morons. If breathing required any sort of thinking, the world would be only half populated!

I know I know... I'm soooo f@cking Zen!

Now, let's not get carried away and pretend that every exhale is like some magical purification ceremony. Nah, mate, you're just blowing out carbon dioxide, which is like the grotty leftovers from your body's late-night kebab binge. Oxygen in, carbon dioxide out—simple as that. No need to summon Vishnu or channel your inner shaman, just breathe like a bloody human being.

And here's the kicker: that oxygen you're sucking in isn't just fuelling your next bicep flex; it's getting distributed like a friggin' VIP pass to all your cells. Your brain cells are doing the Macarena, your muscles are tangoing, and even your gut's having a good ol' jig. You see, your body's like a mini-rave, and oxygen's the DJ that keeps the party going. And don't even get me started on the heart—your own personal rhythm master. It's pumping that freshly inhaled oxygen all over, like Santa Claus tossin' presents at Christmas. Your heart loves oxygen so much, it wouldn't be caught dead without it. Hell, even the heart's got some dignity, I'll give it that.

So, when you're breathing in yoga, you're just doing what your body was built to do. It's like having a grand ol' laugh with your best mates, but instead of busting a gut, you're just giving your body the goods it craves. And here's the best part: you don't have to contort yourself into a human pretzel or dangle from the ceiling like a bat to get the benefits. Nah, just keep it simple and breathe like a regular Joe.

So, there you have it, you yoga rebels. Breathing ain't no mystical journey to the cosmos—it's a basic life hack that even your great-grandma could've mastered. So next time some self-proclaimed yogi tries to sell you a ticket to the cosmic express, just remember to take a deep breath and tell 'em to bugger off. Your body knows what it's doing, and it ain't waiting for some hipster guru to drop knowledge bombs on it. Now, go on, take a breath and get back to your regularly scheduled programming of swearing at traffic and drinking too much tea.

Breathe like a pro

Alright, you eager beavers, listen up for the crash course in deep breathing during yoga poses. Now, don't start picturing yourself soaring like Superman or achieving enlightenment—it's more like getting a teeny-tiny buzz without the booze. Let's dive in, shall we?

Step one: Find yourself a comfortable spot, preferably one where you won't be interrupted by your nosy flatmate or a wandering cat. Sit, stand, or contort yourself like a human pretzel—it's your show, mate.

Step two: Inhale through your nose, like you're snorting the scent of freshly baked biscuits (or whatever tickles your fancy). But hey, don't suck in so hard you end up turning into a human Hoover, alright? Just let the air flow in at its own pace.

Step three: As you're inhaling, imagine that oxygen hitch-hiking its way down to the deepest corners of your lungs, like an explorer on a quest for the lost sock in the laundry. Fill 'em up like you're inflating a balloon with pure, unadulterated air goodness.

Step four: Time to exhale, my friends! Let that carbon dioxide out like it's the punchline to a bad joke. And just like you wouldn't rush through the climax of a gripping drama, don't rush through this exhale. Let it flow out like you're deflating that balloon with all the grace of a slightly tipsy elephant.

Now, onto the real fun—adding this deep breathing jazz to your yoga poses. Let's say you're in the Downward Dog position. As you're hanging out like a tired pup, take a deep breath in, letting your belly balloon out like you've just devoured a five-course feast at the local pub.

Hold it for a beat or two—nothing too dramatic, we're not auditioning for a Shakespearean tragedy. Now, as you're exhaling, let your belly deflate like you've realized you're wearing your underwear inside out in public. Imagine the air leaving your body with the finesse of a deflating bouncy castle.

What's happening, you ask? Well, remember how I mentioned that mini-buzz earlier? Yeah, that's 'cause you're giving your brain a bit of an oxygen hug. It's like your noggin's saying, *"Thanks, mate, I needed that!"* So don't be surprised if you feel a wee bit light-headed, like you've just finished a particularly enthusiastic round of karaoke.

But hold your horses, alright? This ain't your cue to start speaking in tongues or break into interpretive dance. Just ride the wave of that subtle head rush and keep on with your yoga shenanigans. It's like a tiny secret between you and your oxygen-deprived brain—no need to tell the whole bloody universe.

So, there you have it, yoga rebels! Deep breathing ain't some cosmic voyage to a parallel dimension—it's like giving your body a little oxygen high five. No need to overthink it, just inhale, exhale, and carry on with your bendy escapades. Now, go forth and conquer the yoga mat, my slightly light-headed comrades!

Note from the Author: If you are willing to learn how to breath "differently" and get energised, search for a Dutch fella called Wim Hof. They call him The Ice Man (no guys, no Val Kilmer in Top Gun)… anyway, he is a very interesting human but his "way of breathing" really helped me to breath better and get more energised. Try it!

Chapter 7

THE POSES

Alright, you crazy bunch of yoga enthusiasts, get ready for a wild ride through the practical side of this bendy adventure! We've had our fair share of laughs about the mystical mumbo-jumbo, but now it's time to roll out those mats and get serious about twisting and contorting our bodies like we're auditioning for Cirque du Soleil on acid! (Ehehehe, it's gonna be easy don't worry).

But hold your horses, folks! I might just take the piss out of some of these poses, but it's all in good fun. This ain't no pretentious yoga manual, this is a bloody hilarious book of jokes and humour. So don't take it too seriously, because life's too damn short to be all uptight and serious. Who knows, you might kick the bucket tomorrow, so let's loosen up, let's live it up, and let's bloody enjoy this yoga party!

Now let me introduce you to my trusty band of yoga misfits— Mr. YogAvocado and Ms. WineAsana. These yogi-bendy-f@ckers know their moves, and they're gonna show you how to roll like a yoga boss. But remember, ain't no need to go all crazy like a bat outta hell. Listen to your body, find your groove, and let's ride this yoga wave like we mean it.

They'll break down some basics for you, and if you wanna know more about my take on yoga courses, check it out at the end of this ride. But right now, it's all about the action, the laughs, and the good times. So, let's ditch the BS, let's throw away the cosmic crap, and let's get real with this badass yoga adventure!

These three nutters will show you the ropes, or should I say, the yoga mats. Watch 'em move and groove, but remember, don't go flailing around like a drunk flamingo at a ballerina convention. Listen to your body, take it easy, and let the fun flow like a pint of beer on a Friday night. They'll teach you some basic moves, and hey, if you want more wisdom about my thoughts on yoga courses, it's all there at the end of this section. But for now, let's ditch the seriousness, let's chuck away the cosmic mumbo-jumbo, and let's get down and dirty with this hilarious yoga journey!

So, my fellow yogi warriors, grab your mats, stretch those limbs, and let's twist and shout our way through this bonkers yoga adventure! Namas-f@#kin'-Tea, and let's rock this yoga world like never before! Cheers to yoga and laughs, my lovely Yogif@kers!

Meet my trusty helpers: Mr. YogAvocado, and Ms. WineAsana. These three amigos will show you the ropes, or should I say, the yoga mats. Watch them in action, copy their moves, but remember, listen to your body. Don't go overboard like a bull in a china shop. Take it easy, practice, and most importantly, have a bloody good time. They will show you some basics And hey, if you're itching for more information about my suggestion on yoga courses, you'll find it at the end of this section. But for now, let's just enjoy the ride and forget about the serious stuff.

So, my fellow yoga enthusiasts, grab your mats, get ready for some giggles, and let's twist and shout our way through this hilarious yoga adventure! NamasTea, and let's f@#king do this!

Before we dive in, let's get one thing straight—there are like a gazillion yoga poses out there, and trust me, we ain't gonna cover all 84 of 'em. Nah, this isn't some encyclopedia or the holy yoga scripture we're dealing with here. It's a good ol' funny book about yoga, and we're here to have a blast!

So, whether you're a yoga newbie, a seasoned stretchy pro, or somewhere in between, this is the place to be. We'll twist, we'll bend, and we'll find our Zen, all with a pinch of cheekiness and a splash of humour.

NamasTea

No pressure, no judgment—just pure yoga fun!

POSE 1

Cat-Cow | Meow-Muuu

Introducing the Cat-Cow Stretch, or as I like to call it, the Back Cracker Deluxe! This pose claims to be the best for back pain and flexibility, but hey, don't take my word for it—I'm just here for the giggles. According to Dr. Gary Soffer, it's a gentle yet dynamic combo of two poses that's supposed to loosen all your back muscles. Well, who am I to argue with a "cat" and a "cow"?

So, you want to give this a shot? Here's the low-down:

1. Get on all fours, like you're a cat ready to pounce on a pesky mouse.
2. Make sure your wrists are directly under your shoulders and your knees are under your hips. We don't want you collapsing like a Jenga tower.
3. Take a deep breath in and arch your back like a cow, sticking your belly out and puffing that chest up. Feel like a majestic cow grazing on the green pastures.
4. Now, breathe out and become a stealthy cat, round that back, pull that navel in, and let gravity drop your head toward the floor. You're a ninja cat on the prowl.

Repeat this feline boogie as many times as you like. It's like dancing with your spine, a symphony of mobility in your back. And who knows, maybe your joints will be happier than a kid in a candy store.

Remember, this yoga stuff is all about finding what works for you. So if you feel more like a roaring lion or a hissing snake, go ahead, make it your own. Just don't forget to breathe and avoid turning your living room into a zoo.

And hey, if this stretch brings you some relief, well, that's the cherry on top of the cake. So, embrace your inner cat and cow, dance that spine, and let's crack some backs—metaphorically, of course. Let's meow and moo our way to yoga glory!

NamasTea

POSE 2

Downward Facing Dog | Booty Skyward Spine Cracker

Ah, the magical "Downward Facing Dog"! It's like the Swiss Army Knife of yoga poses—versatile, multitasking, and ready to solve all your problems, or so they say. According to Dr. Mukai, it's not just your ordinary stretch—it's a wonder pose that helps with back pain, core strength, and flexibility from head to toe. Wow, it's like a superhero stretch!

Now, let's get into the action, shall we?

1. Plant those hands and knees on the floor like you're about to take off in a rocket ship. Prepare for lift-off!

2. Press the balls of your feet into the ground, and hey, straighten those legs like a majestic pyramid. Who needs the Leaning Tower of Pisa when you have the Downward Facing Dog?

3. Push your hips to the ceiling, and with your shoulders down and back, you'll feel like a proper, fancy yoga table. Just make sure not to go full-on stretchyh

with those knees—no one wants their legs on display at the circus.

And here comes the kicker—let's add some drama! Bend one knee at a time, and whoa, it's like you're in a slow-mo movie scene. Feel the stretch through those hamstrings and calves, like you're a gymnast doing a flawless dismount.

But wait, there's more! This pose promises to take the pressure off your spine, like a mini vacation for your back. It's traction time, baby! And let's not forget about those hamstrings and calves—they get a VIP treatment, like getting a free pass to the yoga spa.

So, if you're looking for a pose that's got it all—strength, flexibility, and a touch of showmanship—look no further than the Downward Facing Dog. It's the yoga rockstar that'll make you feel like a superhero on a mission to conquer the mat. Strike that pose, my fellow yogis, and let's unleash our inner dog! Woof!

POSE 3

Knees to Chest | Bended-Knee Bonanza

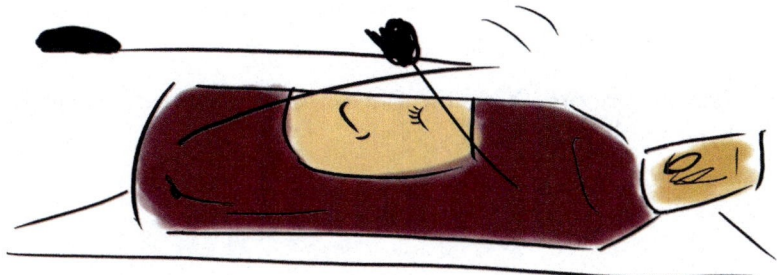

Behold the "Back-Pain-Be-Gone" pose! This yoga masterpiece is here to banish all your back troubles and give you the flexibility of a contortionist with a touch of rock 'n' roll swagger. So, get ready to rock your spine and show off those yoga moves like a rebellious yogi on a mission.

Now, let's break down the steps with a touch of cheeky humour:

1. Picture yourself lying on your back like a boss—hips and knees bent, hands pressed against your knees like you're about to solve some mystical yoga riddle. Oh, the secrets of the universe are just a knee-hug away!

2. Time to unleash your inner drama queen! Exhale like you're releasing all the woes of the world as you wrap those knees in a tight, loving embrace. Navel drawn in, you're practically embracing your inner Buddha with a hint of diva.

3. Inhale like you've just won a yoga Grammy award as you gracefully return to the starting position. A yoga superstar in the making, no doubt!

And guess what? There's a bonus feature! Rock gently from side to side like a cradle for your lower back—because your back muscles deserve a lullaby. It's like giving them a tender massage from the yoga gods themselves.

Dr. Soffer, the yoga sage, says we hold tension in this area—duh, who doesn't? But fear not, dear readers, because this pose is your secret weapon against back-pain villains. It's like Batman swooping in to save Gotham—only with more stretches and less bat gadgets So, the next time back pain tries to crash your yoga party, just whip out the "Back-Pain-Be-Gone" pose and watch it flee like a scaredy-cat. Rock, stretch, and embrace your way to a spine that's ready to conquer the world.

Bravo! Bravo! Encore! Your lumbar deserves a standing ovation! Namaste, my fellow rockstar yogis!

A.S.Salomone

POSE 4

Bridge Pose | Booty Booster Bridge

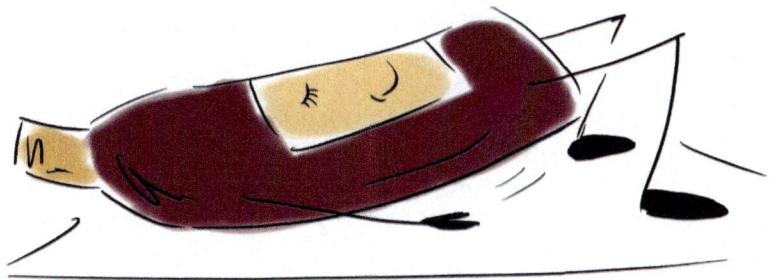

Ladies and gentlemen, brace yourselves for the "Booty Booster Bridge" pose—your one-way ticket to a sculpted core, a back that's got your back, and glutes that could give Beyoncé a run for her money. This pose will have your body singing praises to the yoga gods and your hips doing a victory dance!

Now, let's dive into the hilarious step-by-step guide:

1. Get ready to rock and roll, yogis! Lie on your back like a starfish, arms chilling by your sides, and embrace the cosy floor like it's your own personal yoga throne. Ah, the perks of being a yoga royalty!

2. Next, plant your feet firmly on the ground, hip-width apart. Just imagine you're about to bust some dance moves at a wild yoga party—get those feet ready to groove!

3. Now, squeeze your ass like if you want a crack a wholenut with your glutes take the stage! Engage those superhero muscles and lift your hips like you're about to conquer Mount Everest with your bare hands. Show that gravity who's the boss!

Voila! Your body has now transformed into a straight line from your knees to your shoulders, like a majestic bridge connecting

NamasTea

two mystical lands. The "Booty Booster Bridge" is the ultimate multitasker—it strengthens your core and back, giving your spine a well-deserved break. Take that, back pain!

But wait! This pose also treats your hips like VIPs, stretching those front-of-the-hip muscles that suffer after long Netflix marathons. Now, you can sit for hours guilt-free, knowing that the "Booty Booster Bridge" has your hips' back.

One of the the secret to a strong core and a happy back? This exercise.

You'll feel so powerful that you might just start a "Booty Booster Bridge" fan club. Time to strike a pose, yogis! Embrace your strength, groove to your yoga rhythm, and rock that booty like it's nobody's business. Crotch the sky, my fellow booty-boosting champions!

POSE 5

Cobbler's Pose | Butterfly Effect

Ah, the "Butterfly Effect" pose! A delightful yoga move that's all about bringing those knees together like two long-lost friends catching up for tea. It's like a yoga reunion where your hips get to party and let gravity do all the work.

Let's break down this hip-happy extravaganza:

1. Start with your legs extended in front of you, looking all proper and stiff like a penguin in a tuxedo. But wait! It's time to break free and let loose.

2. Bend those knees, bringing your heels towards your body like you're about to unveil the secret hip party. Oh, the excitement!

3. Now comes the magic part—letting your knees fall out to either side while pressing the soles of your feet together. Voilà! It's like your feet are secret agents on a mission to open up your hips, and gravity is their loyal sidekick.

4. Draw your heels close to your body, but not too close like an awkward yoga Tinder date. Just enough to feel comfortable and cosy like two peas in a pod.

5. Keep that spine elongated, shoulders down, and away from your ears, like a proper yoga posture that knows how to keep its cool even when the party gets wild.

This pose is the key to hip heaven. With knees falling out like a well-choreographed dance move, it's like giving your hips the freedom to dance like nobody's watching. And guess what? It's not just about looking cool in the yoga world. Studies even show that it can work wonders for people with diabetes. Improved total cholesterol, blood glucose, and overall sense of well-being?

That's one fabulous butterfly effect! So, if you want to join the hip party and improve your flexibility, the "Butterfly Effect" pose is your gold ticket. Let your knees drop, feel the magic of gravity, and unleash the hip-tastic adventure. Hip-hip-hooray!

NamasTea

POSE 6

Chair Pose | where's the chair?

Ah, the "Where's the chair" pose, or as I like to call it, the "Buns of Steel" pose! It's like defying gravity, but instead of floating, you're sitting mid-air, working those glutes and back muscles like a boss! Picture this: You're standing there with your feet together, looking all poised and proper. it's time to unleash your inner superhero and channel the power of a squatting warrior!

Here's how you do it, mate:

1. Plant your feet together like they're about to conquer the world in perfect unity. Now, bend those knees and sink your hips back, as if you're about to take a seat in an invisible throne. Yes, an invisible chair that's only for the bravest of yogis!

2. Aim to get those thighs as close to parallel to the floor as possible. It's like doing a gravity-defying squat that challenges

both your upper and lower body strength. Look at you, sitting in thin air like a champion!

3. Keep your knees tracking behind your toes, like a perfectly choreographed dance move that shows off your impeccable form. And don't forget to reach your hips back, giving a nod to that invisible chair that's supporting your yogi glory.

4. Now, here comes the superhero part. Lift those arms up, reaching for the sky like you're about to conquer the universe. Press your shoulders down and away from your ears, because a superhero never slouches!

5. But wait, there's more! If you're feeling extra daring, lift those heels off the ground and find your balance. It's like a daring tightrope walk, except you're floating in mid-air like a yoga wizard!

This "Sit on an Invisible Chair" pose is not for the faint-hearted. It's for those who dare to challenge themselves, who seek to build strength and balance in one magnificent move. So, embrace your inner superhero, feel the burn in your bum, and own that invisible chair like a true yogi boss.

Now, if you ever come across a real invisible chair, you'll be prepared—thanks to the power of yoga! Keep practising, keep squatting, and remember, you're a yoga superhero in the making!

POSE 7

Tree Pose | Drunk flamingo

Alright, folks, brace yourselves for the "Drunk Flamingo" pose, also known as the Tree Pose! It's like trying to stand tall after a night of partying with your feathered friends. Get ready to wobble like a tipsy bird as you channel your inner flamingo!

Here's the deal, my fellow yogi adventurers:

1. Stand up straight, looking all composed and ready to take on the world. Like you've just had a bit too much of that fancy flamingo cocktail!

2. Now, clasp your hands together in the prayer position and lift them above your head, reaching for the stars—or maybe just the ceiling. It's like raising your glass for a toast, but without the actual drink this time.

3. Balance on your right leg, just like a flamingo balancing on one leg while showing off its pink feathers. But be warned, you might sway like a palm tree in a tropical storm!

4. Now, here comes the fun part. Bend your left knee out to the side, bringing your foot to the inner thigh of your right leg. Oh, it's a bit like trying to stand on one leg after a night of dancing, isn't it? But fear not, my tipsy friends, just go with the flow!

5. Hold this pose for a whole 30 seconds. It might feel like an eternity in flamingo years, but you've got this! And remember, if you start teetering like a wobbly bird, just laugh it off and try again—like a true yoga adventurer!

6. Time to switch legs and repeat the wobbly journey on the other side. Embrace the wackiness, embrace the laughter, and embrace the drunk flamingo within you!

Don't be fooled by the name "Drunk Flamingo" pose. It may seem like a silly spectacle, but it's also a fantastic way to stretch your body from head to toe. You'll feel as long and elegant as a flamingo's graceful neck—minus the feathers, of course!

And hey, let's not forget that this wobbly adventure is an excellent opportunity to improve your balance. It's like a game of "flamingo twister," but without the colourful mat!So, my fellow tipsy yogis, embrace your inner flamingo, wobble with grace, and have a blast with the "Drunk Flamingo" pose. Remember, it's not about being perfect—it's about having fun, enjoying the journey, and finding balance.

NamasTea

POSE 8

Cobra pose | Cobra-licius back saver

Ah, the Cobra Pose! It's like a magical potion for your body, offering a whole lot of goodness in a single package. Get ready to unleash the power of the slithery serpent!

Here's the low-down, my fellow yoga explorers:

1. Lie down on your mat, just like a content snake taking a peaceful nap. Now, place your hands under your shoulders, ready to lift yourself up like a majestic cobra rising from the ground.

2. Take a deep breath in, and as you exhale, push your upper body up, arching your back like a true cobra preparing to strike. Feel that delicious stretch in your spine as it strengthens and loosens up—talk about snake magic!

3. But wait, there's more! If you're guilty of slouching like a tired office worker, the Cobra Pose is here to rescue your posture. It's like a gentle reminder to stand tall and embrace the benefits of walking like a confident cobra in the wild!

4. And here's a little secret, whispered among yogis with a wink and a smile: some claim that the Cobra Pose can even grant you a "perky bottom." Yes, you heard that right! It's like a

sneaky bonus, the kind of booty boost that makes you strut like a proud cobra in a yoga class.

So, my slithery friends, embrace the Cobra Pose and let it work its magic. Strengthen your back, loosen up your spine, and say goodbye to slouching. Get ready to rock that perky bottom like the confident cobra you truly are!

But remember, this pose isn't about taking yourself too seriously—it's about enjoying the journey, having fun, and finding the delight in every stretch. So go ahead, hiss like a cobra if you feel like it! After all, in the world of yoga, anything is possible—even a little serpentine charm.

So, strike a pose, feel the stretch, and bask in the glory of the Cobra Pose. Whether you're a seasoned yogi or a beginner exploring the world of yoga, this posture has got your back—and your bottom, too! Happy hissing and stretching, my fabulous yoga adventurers!

POSE 9

Warrior 2 | Fierce Frying Pan

Ladies and gentlemen, gather 'round for the majestic "Warrior 2" pose, or as I like to call it, the "Fierce Frying Pan" stance! Imagine you're a kitchen warrior, ready to flip pancakes with the intensity of a fearless gladiator. Time to unleash your spatula – I mean, sword – and prepare for breakfast battles like never before!

So here's the recipe for the "Fierce Frying Pan" pose:

1. Stand tall like you're about to conquer your kitchen domain. Imagine you're about to flip an epic pancake of courage.

2. Step one foot back like you're doing a stealthy retreat from the pancake battlefield, and lunge the other foot forward. Your stance should be as wide as a breakfast buffet spread.

3. Stretch your arms out parallel to the ground, one in front of you and one behind you. It's like you're gracefully flipping pancakes in both directions. Just remember, in this battle, the only thing sizzling is your determination!

4. Turn your head to look over the front arm, as if you're spotting the next pancake that needs flipping. Or maybe you're just imagining a stack of golden pancakes waiting for your triumphant return!

5. Stay in this pose and feel the burn in your legs, just like you'd feel the heat from a sizzling pan. But don't worry, you're not cooking – you're conquering!

6. After a warrior-worthy interval, switch to the other side and repeat the pancake-flipping extravaganza. Because why flip just one pancake when you can flip a whole stack of courage!

Now, my fellow pancake warriors, remember that the "Fierce Frying Pan" pose is not just about having a flipping' good time – it's also fantastic for building strength and balance. So embrace your inner kitchen gladiator, flip those imaginary pancakes with gusto, and let your inner breakfast champion shine through! Who knew that pancakes and yoga could make such a fantastic team?

POSE 10

Triangle pose | Triangular Toast

Ladies, gentlemen, and breakfast enthusiasts, welcome to the kitchen of enlightenment, where we're about to cook up a savoury masterpiece known as the "Triangular Toast" pose! Get ready to slice through the morning haze with the precision of a seasoned chef and achieve a state of culinary nirvana like never before.

Here's the recipe for the "Triangular Toast" pose:

1. Step onto your yoga mat with the confidence of a head chef entering the bustling kitchen. You're about to whip up a yoga dish that's as delicious as it is enlightening.

2. Take a wide stance, just like you're buttering a generous slab of your favourite bread. Stretch those arms out to the sides, forming a line as straight and appetizing as a well-laid table.

3. Tilt your torso to one side, as if you're smoothly spreading avocado on that massive slice of toast. Imagine your top hand is a spatula of cosmic wisdom, gliding across the canvas of your life.

4. Extend your other arm towards the sky, reaching for the celestial butter dish. It's like you're adding a sprinkle of stardust to your morning creation.

5. Turn your head to gaze at the lifted hand, as if you're admiring your perfectly toasted work of art. Or perhaps you're just daydreaming about the moment you sink your teeth into the most enlightening breakfast ever.

6. Savour this moment like a fine dining experience. Let the flavours of strength, balance, and flexibility blend together into a symphony of sensation.

7. Just like when you're flipping your toasty treat to achieve the perfect crispiness, switch sides and repeat the process. Because why enjoy just one side of enlightenment when you can have it twice?

So, my fellow gastronomic yogis, remember that the "Triangular Toast" pose isn't just about culinary flair – it's a journey to stretch your body, mind, and taste buds. Embrace your inner culinary artist, slice through the mundane, and toast to a morning of balanced deliciousness. Who knew that yoga could pair so deliciously with breakfast?

Bon appétit and NamasTea!

POSE 11

Child's pose | Mini Nap Master

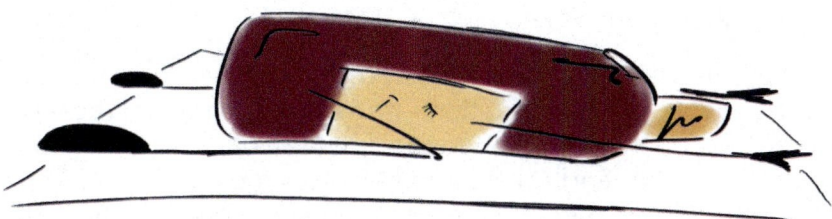

Welcome to the land of Zen and comfort, where we're about to embark on a journey to the "Mini Nap Master" pose, also known as the Child's Pose! Get ready to snuggle up to tranquillity like you've just found the cosiest blanket fort ever.

Here's the delightful recipe for the "Mini Nap Master" pose:

1. Begin by kneeling down, just like you're settling into your favourite nook for a much-deserved nap. Let your big toes touch, and open up your knees wide, creating a comfy little nest for your magical adventure.

2. Slowly lower your torso forward, allowing it to cradle between your thighs. It's as if you're curling up under a blanket that's as soft as a cloud. Tuck those arms alongside your body, like you're giving yourself the warmest of snuggles.

3. Rest your forehead on the ground or on a soft pillow, if you're feeling extra fancy. Imagine this is your personal snooze button, ready to transport you to a realm of tranquillity and rejuvenation.

4. Take slow, deep breaths, letting go of any tensions or to-do lists. It's your very own invitation to chill, recharge, and remind yourself that it's okay to take a break from the busyness of life.

5. Stay in this cocoon of relaxation for as long as you desire, soaking up the cosiness like a cat soaking up a sunbeam.

NamasTea

Imagine yourself drifting off into a dreamland filled with peaceful adventures.

6. When you're ready to rise from your slumber, do so with a gentle stretch, like you're waking up from the most refreshing nap ever. Embrace that renewed energy and carry it with you throughout your day.

Ok, nap enthusiasts, remember that the "Mini Nap Master" pose isn't just about physical relaxation – it's a ticket to a mental vacation. Embrace your inner nap connoisseur, wrap yourself in the warm embrace of calm, and take a moment to simply be. Who knew that yoga could be the ultimate siesta escape? Sweet dreams and namaste!

And there you have it, the grand finale of this epic journey through the wonderland of poses. We've twisted, we've stretched, and we've resembled everything from wandering wildebeests to drunken flamingos. But don't let that fool you, oh no! Beneath the laughter, behind the quirky names, there's a treasure trove of benefits waiting to be unveiled.

Sure, the "Fierce Frying Pan" pose might sound like a f@cking breakfast chef's fantasy, but in reality, it's a muscle-toning, balance-boosting, inner warrior summoning masterpiece. And let's not forget the "Triangular Toast" – who knew toast could be a gateway to enlightenment, right? We've embraced the nap life with the "Mini Nap Master" pose, sneaking in moments of serenity like ninjas of calmness.

Remember, in this topsy-turvy world of yoga, the name might sound absurd, but the benefits are as real as that last bottle of wine in your fridge. And I would never stress it enough to listen to our bodies, to know when to push a bit further and when to take it easy like a sloth on a Sunday afternoon. Yeah, that's right, your body is the boss – treat it like royalty, and it might even reward you with a little extra flexibility.

As we transition from one pose to another, let's not make it look like we've just stepped into a minefield, shall we? Smooth transitions, folks, like sliding into a comfy pair of pyjama pants after a long day. And don't forget the breath – not the "I'm hyperventilating because I lost my TV remote" kind of breath, but the deep, soul-filling inhales and exhales that rejuvenate you from the inside out.

So, raise a glass – or a cup of herbal tea if you're feeling particularly saintly – and let's toast to these poses that have twisted us, turned us, and somehow made us feel oddly alive. Here's to WineAsana, who's not only clarified the poses but also taught us that yoga is as much about celebrating the quirks as it is about nailing the pose.

And now, my fellow warriors, go forth and yogi on, remembering that you're as bendy as a Gumby* doll and as fierce as a caffeine-deprived office worker on a Monday morning. NamasTea, my friends, and remember – keep it bendy, keep it balanced, and keep that laughter flowing like a bottomless glass of wine at a never-ending dinner party. Cheers to you and your gloriously twisted, hilariously balanced journey!

*"Whodda f@ck is Gumby?" most of you would ask... well it' was an American television series of a green clay animation humanoid, it's a thing between a green turd and a celery stick, but very flexible!

More Poses from one and only Mr Yogavocado!

Did you gracefully glide through your workout with the fabulous Ms. Wineasana? If so, you must be radiating pure awesomeness right now! But don't fret, my dear Yogis and Yoginis, because the one and only Mr. Yogavocado is here to introduce youto a delightful array of yoga positions. You can dance from one pose to another, but remember, the golden rule of the yoga realm: always be besties with your body. So, keep it real, relish those stretches, and practice, practice, practice! In no time, you'll be savouring the sweet fruits of your yoga labour!

NamasTea

Triangle Bum up

Sumo phalanges breaker

Lazy crescent lunge

Intricate ballerina

Less intricate ballerina

Praying spider

A.S.Salomone

Drunk flamingo

Joint's heaven

NamasTea

Upside down

Leg up

Human pretzel

Split warrior

NamasTea

Leg up 2

Sciatica paradise

Easy balance

Easy praying flamingo

NamasTea

Sit and chill

Chapter 8

SAVANASTASHAGATAMA THE ULTIMATE YOGA EXPERIENCE

Alright, listen up, you seekers of pseudo-spiritual nirvana! Let's debunk the mumbo-jumbo behind the "oh-so-serious" yoga practice and roll our eyes at its ancient roots.

First off, we got "Savasana", or as I like to call it, "The Ultimate Nap Time." It may look like you're taking a bloody siesta after a sweaty yoga session, but no, my friends, it's a "fully conscious pose"! Yeah, right, as conscious as a sloth on Valium!

So, apparently, you're supposed to lie there like a corpse, which is a bit morbid, innit? The yogi gurus probably had a wicked sense of humour to come up with that one.

Step 1 and only: "Pretend you're dead, but not really." Done? Brilliant!

And what's with all the talk about "assimilating benefits" and "eliminating tension"? It's like they've got their own secret language that they whisper in hushed tones to make it sound all mystical and stuff. "Oh, but the energy, the Chakras, the spiritual alignment!" Pffft, I'm just here to stretch my hamstrings, not join a cult!

But wait, it gets better! Apparently, you're supposed to lie there, closing your eyes and breathing naturally for 10 to 20 minutes. Are they trying to teach us how to nap like pros? I can do that in my sleep—pun intended!

And let's not forget the "powerful benefits" they promise, even if you just do it for a few minutes. Yeah, sure, like I'm going to have some sort of cosmic epiphany in that pose. If anything, I'll probably start dreaming about pizza toppings and unicorns.

So, there you have it, folks—Savasana, the ancient art of playing dead while pretending to be enlightened.

Namaste my arse!

Here there are some very common thoughts while we are practice this amazing pose:

> "Alright, mate, how much bleedin' longer are we stuck in this mind-numbing chat?"

> "Did that bloke just snore or did a long fart? I can't see sh!t from here?"

> "Oi, what's cooking tonight? Fridge is empty... Takeaway! F@ck it!"

> "Did he really dumped me last night? What a piece of sh!t!"

> "Bugger me, I'm starving! My stomach's growling louder than a pack of wild lions. I need some grub, pronto!"

> "What the hell is my life all about, anyway? Is it just a series of random events, or am I supposed to have some grand cosmic purpose? Hello... Universe... I'm here!Mmmhh Nothing!"

> "Did I remember to pay the damn meter? I don't need another parking ticket adding to my collection of bureaucratic crap!"

"Maybe I should just quit my job and tell my boss where to stick it!"

"Did I pick up the kids? Wait ... I don't have any pfffiiuu!"

"My neck hurts, my sciatica is f@cking killing me!... next time I'm gonna buy a voucher on Groupon after a bottle of white I'll open another one and pass-out on the couch instead!"

Those are very common deep and profound thoughts but don't worry my sweet BnB*, I have THE solution for you all. Instead of practice Savasana...

Practice: Savanastashagatama!

C'mon fellas continue this chapter with faith!

Savanastashagatama

Welcome to the mind-boggling, batsh!t crazy world of Savanastashagatama—the ultimate yoga experience that will have you questioning your sanity and laughing your arse off.

What the f@ck is Savanastashagatama, you may ask? Brace yourselves, my fellow seekers of absurdity, as we take you on a wild ride through the most unconventional and downright ridiculous elements of yoga. Get ready to enter the realm of "F@ck it!" yoga attitude!

The Origins of Savanastashagatama

Legend has it that Savanastashagatama was discovered by an ancient yogi who had reached the pinnacle of enlightenment through sheer absurdity. Yeah, this dude realized that true liberation doesn't come from pretentious perfection but from embracing the chaos and randomness of life. And that's how

Savanastashagatama was born—a practice that gives the middle finger to logic and makes you wonder if you've gone bonkers.

The ethimology of Savanastashagatama

After 5 minutes of meticulous researches while on the toilet seat after morning coffee, I can confidently proclaim that the etymology of the word Savanastashagatama can be interpreted as follows:

- "Savanas" refers to a yoga practice that originated in a savanna, taking inspiration from the natural surroundings and embracing the wildness of the environment.

- "Ta" is a nod to the ancient yoga language, specifically from the northern region of the United Kingdom, where practitioners would use "ta" as a way of expressing gratitude and thanks to cosmos.

- "Saga" highlights the need for indulging in a fair share of shaga (a playful term) during the practice, emphasizing the importance of releasing inhibitions and embracing a sense of freedom.

- "Tama" draws from the Italian language, where "ama" translates to "love." By combining it with "tama," the phrase signifies the love and joy that can be found in this unique yoga practice.

With these etymological interpretations, Savanastashagatama encapsulates the essence of practising yoga in unconventional and amusing ways, expressing gratitude, releasing inhibitions, embracing freedom, and finding love and joy in the process.

Trust me, this is all true!

The Practice of Savanastashagatama

Savanastashagatama ain't your run-of-the-mill yoga class, my friends. It's a wild and untamed adventure where traditional poses get twisted, contorted, and sometimes tossed out like yesterday's takeaway. Say goodbye to alignment and precision—here, it's all about going with the flow and surrendering to the absurd.

Imagine a class where everyone dresses like a bunch of nutters—mismatched socks, unicorn onesies, and Viking helmets galore. And picture this, you trying to balance on a f@cking yoga ball while juggling flaming torches! Oh, and did I mention the soundtrack? It's a mash-up of heavy metal, nursery rhymes, and the occasional sound of a squeaky f@cking toy. Bloody madness!

Now:

Step 1: Find Your "Comfy"

Whether you're sitting like you're chilling on your nan's couch, lying down like you've just tumbled out of bed, or balancing on one finger like a circus performer with a cocaine addiction, just find your version of comfy. The goal? To make those yoga poses look like they've been hit with a dose of hilarity.

Step 2: Pizza and Pints, Mate!

Now, let's add a little twist to this Zen cocktail. Grab yourself a slice of pizza – the greasier, the better – and a pint of your favourite brew. Oh, and if you're feeling fancy, make it a cocktail in a coconut shell. Who says enlightenment can't be paired with a bit of gluttony?

Step 3: Inhale the Absurdity

Take a deep breath – not the kind that makes you look all "Zen master," but the kind that says, "I'm about to embrace my inner loony." Inhale like you're about to dive into a barrel of laughs, and exhale like you're blowing out the candles on a cake that's shaped like a rubber chicken.

Step 4: Giggle 'til It Hurts

Now, here comes the fun part. As you find yourself draped over your mat like a damp ragdoll, take a moment to let out a chuckle or a full-blown belly laugh. Remember, we're here to bend and twist our bodies and our sanity, so let those giggles flow like a burst pipe.

Step 5: Pizza Savasana

Alright, mate, time to enter the ultimate relaxation – Savasana, but with a twist. Lay back, pizza slice in hand (watch out for the cheese grease!), and let your body sink into the ground like it's melted into a pool of goofiness and feel the nirvana while tasting the magic slice!

4. The Savanastashagatama Mantra

Every good yoga practice needs a mantra, and Savanastashagatama has one for you, you absolute legends.

Instructions:

-In the position you are after Step 4, lay down on you bed or sit on your favourite couch, or even while you having a dump after days of spicy takeaways... wherever you feel comfortable basically.

- Big F@cking breath in, like when u suck in bong on a Friday night after a shit day at work.

Then repeat Repeat after me:

> *"I release the need for perfection, Embrace the chaos, find f@cking connection. In the realm of absurdity, I dance and play, Savanastashagatama, my F@cking yoga way!"*

-suggestion: while breathing out, in addiction to it, "play" some music IN YOUR HEAD that will help you with the rhythm: from RnB to Punk, Blues, Heavy metal, Polka, Reggae, Ska, Bluegrass, Americana (no jazz folks... it won't work with that cacophony of mix of melodies).

Done!

It's working innit?

The Benefits of Savanastashagatama

Now, you may think this batsh!t crazy practice is just a laugh, but there's method to the madness, my sceptically-raised eyebrows. Savanastashagatama serves up some benefits that'll leave your jaw on the floor:

- Laughter Therapy: Savanastashagatama unleashes your inner f@cking child and lets you laugh like a hyena. Laughing boosts your mood, kicks stress to the curb, and releases those feel-good endorphins. Get ready to have a laughter-induced six-pack and wipe those tears of joy away.

- Unleashing Creativity: Break free from the boring norms of traditional yoga and unleash your f@cking creativity! You're not just a human pretzel; you're a goddamn artist, dancer, or circus performer. Move like a madman and let your imagination run wild, you brilliant friends!

- Embracing Imperfection: In a world obsessed with perfection, Savanastashagatama gives the finger to that sh!t. It's okay to stumble, fall flat on your face, and look like a complete tool while trying something new. Embrace your imperfections, and remember, life's a f@cking blast when you embrace the "F@ck it!" ops, I mean Savanastashagatama moments.

Chant this sh!t with gusto, and feel the liberation as you embrace the unconventional and celebrate your beautifully imperfect self.

And always remember what the great guru Swami Chai-Latte said:

> *"Savanastashagatama is Shaga Shaga, more you Shaga, better your Asana!"*

So, my adventurous and slightly mad yogis, if you're ready to take your practice to a whole new level of absurdity, dive head-first into the f@cking world of Savanastashagatama. Leave your inhibitions at the door, bring your sense of humour, and get ready to laugh, stumble, and discover the joy of embracing the f@cking unexpected. Life's too bloody short to take everything seriously (I will remind you that a lot because many people didn't realised that yet), so let's unleash our inner chaos and roll our eyes at the mystical origins of yoga. F@ck yeah!

Note from the Author: Ancient Yogi from Tuscany called Shalapasta suggested to do it while sipping a nice bottle of Chianti or his famous guru friend Innith from Sussex suggest a local Ale instead.

Chapter 9

DOWNWARD-FACING DRAMA QUEENS

Welcome to the realm of Downward-Facing Drama Queens, the pose where drama unfolds faster than a TV drama. Why the drama queen title, you ask? Well, let's dive deeper into the exaggerated expressions, self-doubt, and fashion choices that make this pose truly fit for the silver screen.

Picture this: you're in a yoga class, minding your own business, when suddenly the instructor calls out, "Now, let's move into Downward-Facing Dog!" All eyes turn to you, and you feel the weight of the entire yoga studio on your shoulders. You position your hands and feet on the mat, and as you lift your hips into the air, a wave of self-consciousness crashes over you. Are you doing it right? Are people judging your form? The f@cking drama begins.

As you settle into the pose, you start to notice the faces around you. Some yogis are giving their best "I'm so Zen" expression imprinted on their annoying Zen-faces, as if they're auditioning for a high-stakes meditation competition. Their eyes are closed, their brows relaxed, and their lips gently curved into a serene smile. It's as if they've unlocked the secrets of the universe and found inner peace, all while holding a pose that looks suspiciously like an upside-down V. You can't help but wonder if they're secretly aliens who have mastered the art of levitation… you hate them all!

Then there are those who have a more intense approach to Downward-Facing Drama Queen. These yogis have brows furrowed with intensity, as if they're attempting to unlock the secrets of the universe with their downward gaze. You half expect them to levitate off the mat or spontaneously combust from the sheer force of their concentration. It's as if they're convinced that if they stare hard enough, the universe will bend to their will and grant them three wishes (preferably involving unlimited yoga pants and an endless supply of vegan chocolate).

And the audible drama? As you hold the pose, you start to hear a symphony of grunts, groans, and sighs around you. It's as if the yoga studio has been transformed into a vocal warm-up session for an avant-garde opera. Some yogis let out deep, guttural sounds that echo through the room, as if they're summoning ancient spirits or perhaps just trying to find their misplaced car keys. Others let out a series of exasperated huffs and puffs, as if the weight of the world is resting on their shoulders in this very moment. And then there are those who, despite their best efforts, can't help but let out a not-so-Zen-like fart during a quiet moment of reflection. Hey, we've all been there. Let's just hope it blends in with the ambient sounds of nature, while in your head suddenly echoing "the sound of silence" of Simon and Garfunkel!

But let's not forget the fashion choices of the Downward-Facing Drama Queens. They come in all shapes, sizes, and ensembles. There's the yogi who shows up in head-to-toe neon spandex, as if they're auditioning for a role in a 1980s aerobics video. They've got the vibrant leg warmers, the fanny pack for their essential oils, and enough sequins to rival a disco ball. Then there's the one who insists on wearing flowy, billowing pants that trail behind them like a yoga cape. We get it, you want to feel like a mystical yoga f@cking superhero, but trust us, you're just one gust of wind away from a serious fashion faux pas. And let's not forget the yogis who accessorize with an array of crystals and gemstones, as if their chakras need a little extra bling to shine.

Hey, if it makes you feel good, rock that crystal necklace with pride. Just be careful not to poke someone's eye out during a particularly enthusiastic Warrior II pose.

But what truly sets the Downward-Facing Drama Queens apart is their ability to turn a simple pose into a full-blown emotional rollercoaster. As you hold the pose, thoughts race through your mind: "Is my hair frizzing? Did I leave the oven on? Should I have gone for the medium instead of the large?" Your inner drama queen comes alive, ready to steal the spotlight and turn a tranquil yoga session into a mental soap opera. Your mind becomes a stage, and every passing thought is an actor vying for the lead role. It's like an episode of "Days of Our Lives" playing out in the confines of your mind, complete with dramatic pauses and intense close-ups.

But don't worry, my fellow drama enthusiasts! Embracing the Downward-Facing Drama Queen within you can actually be quite liberating. Instead of suppressing those dramatic tendencies, let them shine. Throw in a few exaggerated sighs, dramatic eye rolls, and maybe even a little diva-like hair flip during your next yoga class. Who knows, you might just become the star of the studio, attracting an audience of awe-struck yogis who marvel at your ability to transform yoga into a one-person show.

So, the next time you find yourself in Downward-Facing Drama Queen, remember that it's not just a pose; it's an opportunity to unleash your inner theatrics. Embrace the exaggerated expressions, the self-doubt, and yes, even the questionable fashion choices. Let the drama unfold and relish in the absurdity of it all. After all, laughter and a little theatrics are the secret ingredients that make yoga a truly entertaining and enjoyable experience.

So, strike a pose, unleash your inner drama queen, and prepare to dazzle the yoga world with your show-stopping performance in Downward-Facing Drama Queens. Bravo! Let the dramatic saga continue!

Chapter 10

THE GREAT FIVE WARRIORS UNLEASH YOUR INNER BADASS!

Welcome, warriors of humour, to the majestic realm of the Warrior (Princess and Prince) Workout! Prepare to embark on a journey that will awaken your fierce and fabulous side.

We've taken the traditional Warrior poses and infused them with a playful twist, complete with imaginary battles, warrior cries, and a touch of sass. So, strap on your imaginary armour, grab your imaginary sword, and get ready to conquer the world with a smirk and a shimmy!

New Super Poses

Pose 1: Warrior One – "The Fierce Fashionista"

Imagine yourself stepping onto the runway, ready to dominate the fashion scene. Stand with your feet wide apart, toes pointing forward. Raise your right arm in front of you with a graceful flourish, as if presenting your imaginary designer handbag to the adoring crowd. Lift your chin high, exuding confidence and style. Strike a pose that screams, "I'm a warrior, and I look fabulous!" Remember, dear warriors, battlefields can be fashionable too! And trust me, in this fierce ensemble, you'll have your enemies quaking in their boots... or stilettos!

Pose 2: Warrior Two – "The Power Pose"

Visualize yourself standing on the edge of a cliff, ready to unleash your mighty power. Step your left foot back, keeping it straight and firm on the ground. Bend your right knee, ensuring it aligns with your ankle, forming a 90-degree angle. Extend your arms wide, as if gathering all the energy in the universe into your imaginary fingertips. Feel the strength coursing through your body and let out a mighty warrior cry that echoes across the land. Embrace the power within you, my mighty warrior! Let the world know that you're not just here to strike a pose – you're here to conquer and reign supreme! Remember to do not look down in case you are a real idiot to actually do it on the edge of a cliff while you are doing a live reel on Instagram.

Pose 3: Warrior Three – "The Graceful Warrior"

Imagine yourself as a graceful ballerina (full of stamina boys... that's for you!), defying gravity with every move. Stand tall and proud, balancing on your right leg. Extend your left leg behind you, keeping it straight and parallel to the ground. Extend your arms outward, palms facing down, as if you're about to execute a perfect pirouette. Picture your imaginary tutu twirling in the air as you maintain your warrior pose. Remember, my warriors, even in the midst of battle, there's always room for a touch of elegance. Who says warriors can't be fierce and graceful at the same time? Own it, my warrior ballerina!

Pose 4: Warrior Grounded – "The Battle Cry"

Now, my fierce warriors, it's time to let your battle cries be heard! Take a wide stance, feet firmly planted on the ground. Sink into a deep lunge, bending your right knee while keeping your left leg straight and extended behind you. Raise your imaginary sword high above your head, with a fierce expression on your face. Yes you are as cool as Arnold Swartswhatever in CONAN! And now, let out a battle cry that would make even the mightiest warrior tremble. Roar, scream, or let out a primal yell that sends shivers down your spine. Let the world know that you're a force to be reckoned with! Oh, and don't forget to strike a pose that says, "You don't want to mess with this warrior!"

Pose 5: Warrior Savasanasanasasana – "The Royal Rest"

After a fierce battle, every warrior deserves a moment of royal rest. Lie down on your imaginary golden throne, close your eyes, and let your body sink into the ground. Allow your mind to wander to a place of tranquillity and peace. Visualize yourself surrounded by a kingdom of fluffy clouds, basking in the glory of your victorious conquest. Stay in this regal pose as long as you desire, and emerge from it refreshed and ready to conquer whatever comes your way.

Remember, dear warriors, the Warrior Workout is not just about physical strength; it's about tapping into your inner fierceness and embracing your unique power. So, strike a pose, unleash your battle cries, and conquer the world with a twinkle in your eye and a witty remark on your lips.

In the realm of the Warrior Workout, battles are fought with giggles, poses are executed with style, and victory is celebrated with a sassy strut. So, my fellow warriors, embrace the spirit of the Warrior within you, and let your inner badass shine through. The world is your stage, and you're the star of this epic, empowering show! Remember, dear warriors, your power lies not only in the strength of your bodies but also in the sparkle of your spirit. So, go forth, strike your poses with gusto, and conquer the world, one fabulous step at a time!

PART 3

The Extra Yoga Stuff

Chapter 11

THE ULTIMATE YOGA TOOLBOX

Alright, brace yourselves for a bonkers trip through the batsh!t crazy world of yoga props! You've got your frickin' blocks, straps, bolsters, and blankets, all ready to be your whimsical sidekicks on this wild journey. But seriously, who needs this circus act? Let's dive into the absurdity of these so-called "life-changing" props!

Yoga block

Behold the almighty yoga block! This innocent little foam or wooden brick promises to elevate your practice to new heights. Need a boost? Just plop it under your hand, and voila! Suddenly, you're Michael Jordan with the wingspan of a freakin' condor! Want to feel like a yogi god in your backbends? Grab a block, place it just right, and voila! You're now a human pretzel without breaking a damn sweat.

And guess what? It's not just for yoga, oh no! This magical block moonlights as your very own personal phone stand. Because who needs mindfulness when you can multitask your way to enlightenment, right? "Child's pose" is nap-time? Nah, it's Instagram-scrolling time! Why bother escaping reality when you can bring the mindless scroll-fest right onto your yoga mat? Genius, I know! And it has other amazing functions like use it as doorstop, or even a stepping stool to help you reach those elusive high shelves in your kitchen. Talk about versatility!

And that's not all, my friends! This yoga block might as well be the king of paradoxes, because it takes you to "new heights" while keeping you firmly planted on the ground. It's like the damn oxymoron of the yoga world! Elevate your practice, they say, but don't you dare get carried away—literally! It's like trying to fly with one wing clipped—what's the damn point?

So, there you have it—the grand delusions of the almighty yoga block! It's like the Chihuahua that barks like a Rottweiler—small but mighty in its absurdity. But hey, if it helps you reach new "heights" in your practice or gives you an excuse to be glued to your phone, who am I to judge?

Straps

Oh, and let's not forget the "strap-as-a-fashion-accessory" mishaps. You think you're rocking that trendy headband, but instead, you end up with a strap-induced "helmet hair" disaster. Who needs a bad hair day when you can have a bad yoga strap day?

But hey, despite all the comedic chaos, let's give credit where it's due—the yoga strap can be a handy tool for some folks. It's like the comedic sidekick that tries to steal the spotlight but ends up adding a touch of hilarity to your practice. So, next time you reach for that stretchy accomplice, remember to embrace the giggles, the twisted contortions, and the occasional strap mishaps. After all, yoga is all about finding joy in the journey, even if that journey involves a few stretchy f@ck-ups along the way!

This innocent-looking piece of fabric thinks it's got the power to turn you into a f@cking contortionist. the "super-duper flexi-friend" that promises to turn you into a human pretzel without breaking a sweat! Let's be real, folks, this thing is like the "wannabe contortionist kit" for those of us who never got that elusive invite to Cirque du Soleil. Need help touching your toes? Grab that strap, and suddenly, you're Mr. Fantastic from the Fantastic Four, reaching for the moon! But hey, watch out for the twisty-tornado of pain, because when that sh!t snaps, you won't be doing any yoga for a week. Ouch!

"strapping" accidents? Are always around the corner.

Picture this: you're in a yoga class, trying to look all Zen and graceful while reaching for your toes. You think, "Hey, I'll just loop this damn strap around my feet and voila! I'm a yoga superstar!" But instead of gracefully touching your toes, you end up tangled like a f@cking spaghetti monster in a bowl of marinara sauce. It's like a twisted version of "The Matrix" with you dodging your own limbs!

And when the strap suddenly decides to wage war on your unsuspecting fellow yogis? You're peacefully flowing through your practice when—whack!—the damn strap snaps like a rubber band, launching itself straight into the person next to you. Congrats, you're now a f@cking yoga ninja with a dangerous weapon of stretchy destruction!But the fun doesn't stop there! Oh no, let's talk about the infamous "strap-assisted inversions" gone wrong. You think you're about to gracefully lift your legs into a headstand, but instead, the strap decides to become your personal bungee cord, sending you flinging backwards like a human slingshot. It's like a circus act without the safety net—just pure hilarity and a lot of startled faces! Be careful of that nasty little f@ckers!

But why stop there? With a few loops and twists, your yoga strap can become a stylish headband, a chic belt, or even a makeshift jump rope for those impromptu cardio sessions. Who knew a simple strap could add such pizazz to your yoga practice and your fashion game? Wrap that strap around your head, and voila! Instant fashionista, and now you're rocking a headband that even Lady Gaga would envy. Need a belt to hold up those saggy yoga pants? Strap it around your waist, and voila! Your Dolce e Gabbana style is served! You're a yogi fashion icon with a strap-licious twist!

Bolster

Yeah, the bolster—an overrated, fluffy sidekick that's always trying to cosy up to you like a damn clingy ex. It's like a yoga pillow on steroids, forcing a suffocating bear hug on you when all you want is some damn personal space. But hey, it's not just a yoga prop, oh no, it's the king of DIY forts in your living room! Forget the damn furniture; the bolster's got you covered with its fortress-building skills.

Just add some blankets and pillows, and boom—you've got yourself a cushioned kingdom fit for a yoga-obsessed monarch. Yeah the bolster—an overrated, fluffy supportive friend that's always there for you when you need a little extra cushioning and comfort. It's like a yoga pillow that gives you a big, warm hug, but in reality it could transform in a suffocating ex trying to hug you when you need damn space! But let's be honest, the bolster is not just for yoga.

Oh no, it's so much more. It's the perfect prop for constructing epic fortresses in your living room, complete with blankets and pillows for added cosiness. It can be a makeshift throne for your imaginary kingdom for a yoga-obsessed monarch, or a comfortable seat for your furry friends who insist on joining your practice. And let's not forget its hidden talent—it makes an excellent prop for yoga-inspired Rube Goldberg machines. Just line up a row of bolsters, add a few blocks, and watch as your yoga props cascade and tumble in a perfectly choreographed sequence. It's a yoga practice and a spectacle all in one!

Blanket

Simple... It's a F@CKING BLANKET! That's all BnB*! supposedly a versatile tool that keeps you warm, but let's face it, it's just a frickin' piece of fabric!

Yeah, it adds a touch of whimsy to your practice but don't get me wrong; I love a good superhero movie, but pretending your blanket is a damn cape or magic carpet is a whole new level of delusion. You're not Superman, and you're definitely not Aladdin, so get back to reality! But wait, there's still one more prop to discuss—the mighty yoga blanket. Ah, the blanket—a versatile tool that keeps you warm, offers extra padding, and adds a touch of whimsy to your practice. It's not just a blanket; it's a cape, a magic carpet, or even a superhero's secret hiding place. Need a little extra warmth during Savasana? Snuggle up in your cosy yoga blanket and let the peaceful calm wash over you. Want to add an element of surprise to your practice? Use your blanket to create your very own yoga-inspired "Peek-a-boo" routine. Imagine the delight on your fellow yogis' faces as you pop out from beneath your blanket, striking a pose with a mischievous grin. It's all part of the enchantment of the yoga blanket.

Ah, can you believe this bloody blanket, eh? Claiming cosmic superpowers, all the way from some mystical Indian god-knows-where! For a mere £27.99 on Amazon (f@cking expensive though), this magical fabric vows to transform ye into the goddamn "God of Yoga." It's like the holy grail of enlightenment, wrapped in a cheap piece of cloth! I mean, talk about a f@cking bargain!

Picture this: you're snuggled up in your bargain-blanket, ready to embrace the "cosmic energy" that's supposed to elevate your yoga game. But instead of becoming a yoga deity, you end up looking like a befuddled yogi wrapped in a damn burrito. Och, who needs cosmic superpowers when ye can be a yoga-inspired taco, right?

And let's not forget the "blanket-induced enlightenment" gone wrong! They say this enchanted fabric will lead you on a journey to nirvana, but instead, it takes ye on a wild goose chase to cloud nine. It's like following a treasure map that leads to a f@cking McDonald's drive-thru—disappointing and full of empty promises!

This "blanket of transformation" might as well be a cursed artefact from an ancient temple. Ye think it's adding mystical charm to your practice, but in reality, it's got the supernatural ability to attract every damn dog hair within a five-mile radius! Congratulations, your blanket's now a f@cking furry pet bed.

So do you really believe this magical shroud is gonna make you a "God of Yoga"? Well, let me tell you, it's like thinking a rusty bike will turn ye into the next Tour de France champion! Och, there's no shortcut to enlightenment, my friend. Way better off spending your cash on a pint and a laugh with your friends.

Yoga mats

Yoga mats, guys here we gonna spend a bit more time with this almighty-piece-of- energy-trapping-mystical-force-of-cosmic-nature-thing!

The majestic Aladdin's rag of the yoga world! They sell us this grand illusion of comfort and serenity, but let's face it: they're nothing more than thin, overpriced sponges drenched in sweat and tears from the agony of those godforsaken yoga poses.

You unroll your cosmic mat, believing it'll transport you to a realm of Zen and enlightenment. But as soon as you plant your feet on it, you feel like you've landed on a bed of nails. "Oh, it's just extra grip," they say. Well, I'd rather grip onto the edge of a cliff than subject my poor feet to this torture!

And let's talk about the size, shall we? They call it a "standard" size, but for who? Hobbits? Gnomes? My lanky limbs are spilling over the edges like an overstuffed sausage. It's more like a postage stamp than a yoga mat! And don't get me started on the width. It's like they expect us to fold ourselves into origami masterpieces just to fit!

Oh, and the smell!!If you've ever stepped foot into a yoga studio, you've probably witnessed the hushed reverence with which practitioners treat their yoga mats. It's as if these humble pieces of cushioning have secret powers capable of channelling ancient energies, aligning chakras, and transforming your downward dog into a mystical experience. But is there any scientific evidence to support these claims? Let's find out!

First things first, let's examine the materials used to make these allegedly enchanted mats. Many yoga mats are made from PVC, which stands for Polyvinyl Chloride. Now, PVC is known for its durability and ability to withstand various yoga poses, but magical energy sponges? I think not. If anything, these mats are more likely to absorb sweat and the occasional carpet fuzz than any cosmic vibrations.

Some mats claim to be made from natural materials like cork or natural rubber, adding an extra layer of mystique to their already elusive reputation. But let's not get carried away here. Cork is great for sealing wine bottles, but transforming your warrior pose into an interdimensional experience? Highly unlikely. And as for natural rubber, it's a fantastic material for erasers, but I wouldn't put my spiritual salvation in its hands—or should I say, in its rubbery grip. You'd think you were doing yoga in a chemical factory. What do they put in these things, eau de landfill? It's like downward dogging in a toxic waste dump. Namaste, my ass!

Many yoga mats boast textured surfaces, claiming to enhance grip and stability during practice. Some even claim to have special alignment markings to help you find your perfect pose. Well, I hate to break it to you, but those markings are more like guidelines from a treasure map leading you to the elusive "comfort zone" rather than mystical coordinates on the cosmic grid. And the grip-enhancing texture? It's just there to prevent you from slipping and sliding around like a clumsy seal. It's not an ancient energy force field, folks.

And here's the best part – cleaning it! They say it's easy to clean, but have you ever tried scrubbing dried sweat and tears from a sponge? It's like trying to erase your ex's tattooed name from your arm with a toothbrush. A never-ending battle against the forces of biohazard.

So there you have it, folks. Yoga mats – the cosmic mirage of tranquillity, the sponge of suffering, the toxic waste dump of aromas. Next time you roll out that deceptive piece of foam, remember, it's not a magic carpet ride to serenity. It's just another overhyped accessory trying to cash in on our quest for inner peace. Namaste, my arse again!

Alright, my sweet BnB*. We've covered the yoga block, strap, and bolster, but now it's time to unleash the absolute madness with some outrageous, never-before-seen yoga props. Get ready to stretch your imagination and your sides as we dive into the whimsical world of the NEW yoga products!

Here they are:

"Yog-Tea" Cup Holder

Tired of balancing your cup of chai while flowing through poses? Say hello to the "Yog-Tea" Cup Holder—a revolutionary device that keeps your tea, coffee, or smoothie within arm's reach during your practice. With a handy adjustable grip, you can sip and stretch without spilling a drop. It's the perfect way to fuel your inner yogi and get that caffeine fix in style!

"Om-Matic" Meditation Pillow

Struggling to find your zen in this chaotic world? The "Om-Matic" Meditation Pillow is here to save the day! This high-tech cushion uses soothing vibrations and tranquil melodies to guide you into a state of pure bliss. Just sit back, relax, and let the "Om-Matic" lead you on a cosmic journey to inner peace. It's meditation made easy, my friends!

"Yog-Float" Anti-Gravity Mat

Say goodbye to downward dog, and hello to upward float! The "Yog-Float" Mat uses cutting-edge anti-gravity technology to elevate your practice to new heights—literally. With the touch of a button, you'll defy gravity and experience yoga poses like never before. It's like practising yoga on the moon, minus the spacesuit!

"Yog-Strum" Harmonious Guitar Strap

Who said you can't strum and stretch at the same time? The "Yog-Strum" Guitar Strap is here to unleash your inner rock-star during your practice. Strap on your guitar, strike a pose, and let the music flow as you flow through yoga sequences. It's the perfect union of music and movement that will make you feel like a yoga-shredding maestro!

"Yog-Tail" Balance Enhancer

Tired of wobbling in tree pose? The "Yog-Tail" Balance Enhancer is your secret weapon! This revolutionary tail-shaped device helps you find your centre and achieve perfect balance. Channel your inner cat, wag that tail, and conquer every balance-challenging pose with ease. It's the ultimate tool for balance, flexibility, and adding some extra flair to your practice!

"Enlightenment Earmuffs"

Yes, you heard it right. These stylish and utterly ridiculous earmuffs are specially designed to filter out all distracting sounds and ensure a perfectly serene yoga experience. With the Enlightenment Earmuffs snugly fitted over your ears, you can blissfully ignore any outside noises, whether it's the neighbour's lawnmower, your partner's off-key singing, or even the sound of your own grumbling stomach. Achieving inner peace has never been so fashionable!

"Mystical Magic 8 Ball Mat"

Imagine a yoga mat that not only supports your physical practice but also offers sage advice and mystical insights. With the Mystical Magic 8 Ball Mat, every pose becomes a divination session. The secret is in the very fine magic powder in the Magic 8 Ball Mat! Simply rest your hand on the designated spot, ask a burning question about your life, deeply breath in couple of times and wait for the mat's wisdom to be revealed. Will you find true love? Will you achieve world peace? The answers lie within the realm of the mystical mat. Just don't be surprised if the responses are as enigmatic as a Zen riddle.

There you have it, folks—the NEW yoga products that will revolutionize your practice and unleash the absurdity in every pose. Embrace the hilarity, let your imagination run wild, and remember to have a good laugh along the way. Yoga is not just about finding stillness; it's about exploring the joy, creativity, and downright weirdness that life has to offer. So, grab those blocks, straps, bolsters, and of course, your NEW yoga props, and let's embark on a journey of yoga hilarity like no other.

NamasTea my daredevils yogi!

Chapter 12

YOGA IN THE DIGITAL AGE

Welcome to the world where yoga meets technology, and Instagram filters become our asanas! In this chapter, we embark on a hilarious exploration of how technology and social media have infiltrated the realm of yoga, taking us on a journey through the absurd and exaggerated scenarios that arise when people prioritize likes over inner peace.

Picture this: a yogi strikes a pose, contorting their body into an intricate position not for the sake of their practice, but purely for the pursuit of the perfect Instagram photo. They contort themselves into unimaginable shapes, risking their own comfort and sanity, all in the name of a few more double-taps from their followers. We laugh, we cringe, and we wonder if the ancient sages ever anticipated such a twist in the yoga journey. How many morons are like that on the internet? Thanks to Buddha MILLIONS!

Instagram

Ah, the f@cking Instagram yogis, a splendid circus of characters putting on a bloody show for the digital masses! We've got the wannabe yogis who can't even touch their f@cking toes, but oh bollocks, they'll attempt a headstand just for the likes. Bless their hearts, they're trying, even if they end up tangled in a yoga pretzel of confusion.

Then there are the super gurus, the self-proclaimed masters of f@cking Zen, gracing us with their divine presence on our feeds. They'll strike a pose on a bloody mountaintop, claiming to be one with nature, but in reality, they're just one with their f@cking phone's camera timer. NamasTea, indeed!

Oh, and let's not f@cking forget the Insta-hotties, turning yoga into a f@ckink +18 magazine shoot. We're not sure how those skimpy outfits enhance their practice, but hey, it's all about those heart-eye emojis, right? Yes, but with a f@cking side of steamy seduction.

And how about those who unconsciously make fun of themselves? The ones who try to balance on one bloody hand but end up flat on their faces, or attempt a graceful backbend but look more like a crumpled accordion. We salute their bravery, and their sense of humour, even if it's accidental.

Instagram reels are the playground of the absurd, where yogis defy gravity and logic. They'll spin, flip, and flop, all in the name of being nd viral. The real challenge is deciphering whether it's a yoga pose or a contemporary dance routine. Modern f@cking art, anyone?

In this digital circus, yoga has taken a wild turn, with each scroll bringing a new freacking spectacle. So, let's raise our phones and toast to the Instagram yogis, the digital acrobats, and the unintentional comedians. They may be a colourful bunch, but amidst the madness, they bring laughter and a few head shakes to our bloody day. Keep scrolling, my friends, and enjoy the show!

Apps

In this digital era, yogis become obsessed with tracking every aspect of their practice through apps and gadgets. From counting their breaths to measuring the angle of their bends, yoga becomes a game of numbers and statistics. The serene ambiance of the studio is replaced by beeping gadgets and blinking lights as yogis attempt to reach their daily yoga goals, sometimes forgetting the very essence of the practice itself.

Oh, bloody hell, welcome to the digital f@cking era of yoga, where yogis are hooked on apps and gadgets like it's a massive addiction! They're not just contorting their bodies; they're also twisting their minds with numbers and statistics. It's like they're in a f@#kin' yoga competition with themselves, tryin' to outdo their own breath counts and bend angles.

The once serene ambiance of the yoga studio is now filled with beeps and bleeps, as if we're at a f@#king techno rave instead. They're on a mission to reach their daily yoga goals, and nothin' will stand in their way – not even their own f@cking sanity.

Who needs to connect with their inner peace and breath when you can have an app tell you how to do it, right? Just follow the algorithm, and voila, you're a f@cking yogi guru! Oh, bugger off! Yoga is about finding balance and connection, not being a slave to gadgets and blinking lights.

But hey, let's not forget to check our heart rates and calorie burn while we're at it! Because apparently, it's not enough to just do the poses; we gotta make sure we're burning enough calories to earn that extra slice of cake later. Priorities, people!

In this digital circus of yoga, the gadgets have become the ringmasters, and the yogis are just dancing to their tunes. It's like The Matrix, but instead of dodging bullets, they're dodging their own bloody selves!

So, let's raise a glass to the digital yogis, the ones who've traded in their inner peace for data points and achievements. Keep tracking those breaths, bending those angles, and chasing those goals, because the gadgets demand it! Namaste, my BnB's digital warriors!

Virtual Yoga

Let's not forget the virtual yoga classes, where yogis gather via video calls to flow through poses from the comfort of their own homes. But in this digital landscape, things can get hilariously chaotic. Picture a yogi's cat strolling across the mat

mid-pose, or a participant accidentally muting themselves but continuing to follow along with the class in blissful ignorance.

Oh, bloody brilliant! Welcome to the virtual yoga classes, where yogis gather from the comfort of their own homes to flow through poses like a bunch of digital acrobats. It's like a f@cking circus, but instead of tents, we've got Zoom screens.

Picture this: you're in the middle of a serene pose, finding your Zen, and suddenly, a bloody furry intruder strolls across the mat like it owns the place. Cat-astrophe, anyone? But hey, who needs a calm and peaceful environment when you can have a feline yoga assistant, right?

And that's not all! In this digital wonderland, we've got participants accidentally muting themselves, creating a symphony of silence while the class carries on. They're blissfully unaware of their own f@ck-up, but we're all having a right laugh watching the chaos unfold.

It's like a comedy show, but instead of scripted jokes, we've got real-life bloopers happening in real-time. It's the virtual version of "You've Been Framed," yoga edition!

But hey, who needs perfection when you can have a bit of chaos, right? Life's too short to take yourself too seriously, especially in the digital yoga circus. So, embrace the unexpected, laugh at the mishaps, and keep flowing through the poses, even if it means dodging cat butts and muting yourself.

In this digital landscape, the only certainty is uncertainty, and that's bloody fine. So, let's raise a glass to the f@cking virtual yogis, the ones who've embraced the chaos and found their Zen in the midst of it all.

Yoga Influencer

Ah, the f@cking yoga influencers, the social media circus performers of the yoga world! They're like a bunch of bloody peacocks, strutting around in their flashy poses and designer yoga gear, trying to make us mere mortals feel inadequate with their picture-perfect Instagram posts.

They've got more hashtags than there are stars in the sky, and they're always on the hunt for the next trend to jump on like a bunch of yoga band-wagoners. One day it's goat yoga, the next day it's beer yoga, and who knows what's next? Maybe yoga with llamas or yoga in space!

But let's be real for a moment, are these influencers truly guiding us on a path of self-discovery, or are they just leading us down a rabbit hole of yoga fads? I mean, who needs authenticity and meaningful practice when you can have likes and followers, right?

They've turned yoga into a sh!t popularity contest, where the one with the most followers wins the crown of "Ultimate Yoga Influencer." It's like high school all over again, but instead of prom queen, we've got the yoga king or queen of Instagram.

And let's not forget their flashy poses. They twist and bend themselves into pretzel-like shapes, all for the sake of getting that perfect shot. It's like they're auditioning for a role in Cirque du Soleil, not practising yoga for the love of it.

But hey, who needs inner peace and self-discovery when you can have a million likes, right? They're too busy curating their Instagram feed to bother with real, meaningful practice. It's all about the image, the brand, and the illusion of perfection.

So, my fellow yogis, let's not be fooled by the flashy poses and the catchy hashtags. Let's not get swept away by the circus act of the yoga influencers. Instead, let's focus on our own practice, our own journey of self-discovery, and f@#k the trends and the popularity contest.

Yoga is not a f@cking show; it's a personal journey of growth, self-awareness, and inner peace. So, let's turn off the Instagram filter and embrace the messy, imperfect, and authentic practice of yoga. Let's be real, let's be true to ourselves, and let's find our own path to self-discovery, without the need for flashy poses and a million likes. NamasTea, my fellow authentic yogis!

As we navigate this brave new world of digital yoga, it's important to remember that the true essence of the practice lies not in the number of followers or the perfect yoga selfie, but in the connection we cultivate with ourselves and others. While technology can be a valuable tool for spreading knowledge and connecting with fellow yogis, it's essential to maintain a sense of balance and authenticity amidst the digital noise.

So, dear yogis, let us not fall prey to the lure of likes and the never-ending pursuit of virtual validation. Let us laugh at the absurdity of yoga in the digital age and find solace in the genuine moments of connection and growth that arise when we put down our phones and truly immerse ourselves in the practice.

Remember, yoga is not about the perfect filter or the flawless pose—it's about embracing the imperfections, finding joy in the journey, and nurturing the relationship between mind, body, and spirit. So, next time you feel the temptation to contort your body for the perfect shot or obsess over your yoga stats, take a deep breath and remember the true purpose of yoga: to find peace, presence, and joy along the way.

In this digital age, let us use technology as a tool to enhance our practice, but never forget that the essence of yoga lies within ourselves, not within the glowing screens of our devices. Embrace the imperfections, celebrate the moments of hilarity, and stay true to the heart of yoga, both on and off the digital mat!

Chapter 13

YOGA ETIQUETTE: NAVIGATING THE DO'S AND DON'TS WITH A WINK

Ah, the amazing world of yoga etiquette - a right laugh, innit? Now, listen up, you lot, 'cause we're about to dive into the dos and "don't-s" of this whole yoga shebang, but with a bloody humorous twist. So grab your mats and get ready for a proper good time, ya wankers!

DO: arrive on time, but don't be surprised if the instructor is still f@cking setting up their own mat. 'Cause, you know, they're the masters of yogic time management and all that bollocks.

DON'T: Audibly sigh when someone sets up their mat too close to yours. We know you prefer your personal space, but remember, yoga is all about unity and connection. So, embrace the opportunity to share your energy with your fellow yogis, ya selfish pricks.

DO: Bring your own mat, but don't be afraid to rock that colourful and eye-catching pattern. Who said yoga mats have to be boring as f@ck? Let your mat be a reflection of your vibrant personality. Just be prepared for others to secretly envy your stylish choice.

DON'T: Apologize profusely if you accidentally fart during class. Hey, it happens to the best of us. Embrace it as a sign of releasing negative energy and move the fuck on. After all, there's no use crying over spilt milk—or in this case, spilt gas.

DO: Respect the bloody sometimes-annoying silence in the studio, but feel free to unleash your inner laughter if something funny happens. Laughter is the best medicine, even in yoga class. Just make sure your giggle fit doesn't turn into a full-blown comedy show, stealing the spotlight from the instructor.

DON'T: Hog all the props for yourself. Sharing is caring, and those blocks and blankets are there for everyone's comfort. Plus, you never know when your fellow yogi might need an impromptu fort or a prop for their imaginary yoga-inspired Rube Goldberg machine.

DO: Listen to your body and modify poses as needed, but feel free to add your own f flair and interpretive dance moves. Who says tree pose can't include a graceful sway of the arms or a spontaneous jazz hand flourish? Be your own yoga maestro, ya legends.

DON'T: Judge others for their unique interpretations of poses. So what if your neighbour's downward dog looks more like an upside-down flamingo? Each body is beautifully unique, and yoga is all about embracing our individual journeys.

DO: Hydrate before, during, and after class, but don't be alarmed if your water bottle becomes a makeshift percussion instrument during class. That's just the f@cking universe adding a rhythmic soundtrack to your practice. Embrace the beats and go with the flow.

DON'T: Take yourself too bloody seriously. Remember, yoga is meant to bring joy and lightness to your life. So laugh at your wobbles, embrace your quirks, and let go of any self-judgment. The more you can embrace the fun and playfulness of yoga, the deeper your practice will become.

DO: Support your fellow yogis by giving them a gentle pat on the back when they nail a challenging pose. However, be cautious not to mistake their back for a bongo drum. Let's keep the congratulatory gestures non-percussive, shall we?

DON'T: Engage in intense conversations during Savasana. While it may be tempting to discuss last night's reality TV episode or that juicy gossip, remember that Savasana is a sacred time for relaxation and rejuvenation. Save the chit-chat for the post-yoga brunch and give everyone some peace, ya gabby bastards.

DO: Respect the instructor's expertise, but don't be afraid to challenge their unconventional cues. When they ask you to imagine yourself as a majestic swan floating on a serene lake, feel free to channel your inner flamingo instead. After all, who wouldn't want to strike a pose as fabulous as a flamingo?

DON'T: Engage in unnecessary yoga battles over the prime spot by the window. Sure, natural light is lovely and all, but it's not worth starting a war with your fellow yogis. Remember, the sun shines on everyone, so find your inner glow regardless of where you're positioned in the room.

DO: Embrace the post-yoga glow, even if it leaves you looking like you just ran a marathon in a sauna. Sweat is a sign of hard work and dedication, so wear that sweaty badge with pride, ya sweaty bastards.

DON'T: Get caught up in stupid yoga fashion wars. Yes, there are some fancy yoga outfits out there, but let's not lose sight of the purpose of yoga. It's not a runway show, and you don't need to bankrupt yourself to look the part. A comfy t-shirt and some stretchy pants will do just fine.

DO: Be mindful of your f@cking drishti (gazing point) during class, but don't get so fixated on it that you end up staring down your neighbour. It's not a staring contest, ya creepy bastards.

DON'T: Be a bloody yoga snob and look down on others who are just starting their yoga journey. We were all beginners once, and it's important to be supportive and encouraging to those who are new to the practice. We all fall over in tree pose at some point, so let's share a laugh and a helping hand, ya compassionate souls.

DO: Remember that yoga is not just about physical poses. It's a holistic practice that includes breath-work, meditation, and a whole lot of self-discovery. So don't be afraid to dive into the depths of your mind and soul during your practice. Who knows what treasures you'll find in there?

DON'T: Use yoga as a f@cking excuse to show off your flexibility or strength. It's not a competition, and there's no gold medal for the most advanced pose. Yoga is about inner growth and self-awareness, not impressing others with your circus-like contortions.

DO: Embrace the wobbles and tumbles during your practice. We all have off days, and there's no shame in stumbling out of a pose or losing your balance. It's all part of the journey, so laugh it off and keep on flowing, ya resilient souls.

DON'T: Take yourself too seriously. Yes, yoga is a beautiful and transformative practice, but that doesn't mean you have to be a solemn monk during every bloody class. Crack a smile, have a laugh, and remember that life is too short to be f@cking sober all the time.

So, dear yogis, let's navigate the world of yoga with a playful spirit and a smile on our faces. Embrace the dos and don't-s as gentle reminders, but don't forget to infuse your practice with laughter, authenticity, and a dash of light-heartedness. After all, yoga is about finding balance in both body and spirit, and what better way to achieve that than with a little humour?

NamasTea, ya cheeky f@ckers!

Chapter 14

THE MYTHICAL ZEN ACCIDENTS, FROM SLIPS N SLIDE TO FARTS N BURPS.

Oh, you thought the fart and burp show was the only funny accident that could happen during a yoga class? Think again, my friends! Yoga is a playground for all sorts of hilarious mishaps and moments that will leave you in stitches. Here's a list of other side-splitting accidents you might encounter:

Slit and Slide

Alright, buckle up, my fellow yogis, because we've got a slippery situation on our hands! Picture this: You're in the middle of a serene yoga class, gracefully flowing from pose to pose like a majestic swan. But little do you know, your hands and feet have decided to throw a wild party, and it's about to get wet and wild!

As you move into Downward Dog, your hands become supercharged with sweat, turning your trusty yoga mat into a Slip 'n Slide extravaganza. Oh, the joy! You gracefully plant your feet on the mat, thinking you've got this yoga thing down. But little did you know, your feet have teamed up with your hands for the ultimate surprise.

Just as you lift your hips and press back, your feet decide to join the sweaty shindig, making your mat as slippery as a greased-up pig at a country fair. Suddenly, you find yourself slipping and sliding, trying to hold your pose but failing miserably. It's like doing yoga on an ice rink, but without the fun of ice skates.

The yoga instructor calls out "Hold it, hold it!" as if you're participating in some Olympic event, but it's more like a chaotic game of Yoga Twister. Your arms flail in one direction, while your legs go off on a tangent of their own. It's a circus act in the making!

You try to regain your balance, but it's a lost cause. Your fellow yogis look on in both horror and amusement as you become the star of the Slip 'n Slide Show. You can almost hear the circus music playing in the background as you attempt to gracefully land back on your mat.

But alas, your mat has become a dance floor of its own, and you find yourself doing the Yoga Cha-Cha, sliding from one end to the other. It's like a comedy sketch brought to life, and you can't help but burst into laughter at the absurdity of it all.

The yoga instructor, trying to keep a straight face, offers some words of encouragement, but it's hard to take anything seriously when you're the star of the Slippery Yoga Olympics. You try to find your inner Zen, but it's drowned out by the sound of your fellow yogis snickering and trying to stifle their giggles.

Eventually, the Slip 'n Slide party comes to an end as you gracefully crash onto your mat, covered in sweat and laughing like a maniac. You may not have mastered the pose, but you've definitely mastered the art of comedy on a yoga mat.

Next time you hit the yoga mat, beware of the Slip 'n Slide surprise waiting for you. Embrace the hilarity, embrace the absurdity, and most importantly, embrace the joy of laughing at yourself. After all, yoga is not just about perfect poses, but about finding the humor in the imperfect moments. Namaste, my slippery warriors!

Farts n burps

OK guys I left this as last because it's funny and f@cking embarrassing… c'mon you, I know that happen to you before! The glorious yoga sessions where our bodies decide to perform their own symphony of farts and burps! Get ready, you cheeky buggers, 'cause we're diving deep into the world of bodily noises in this hilariously sarcastic chapter.

Picture this: you're in the midst of a serene yoga class, all Zen and shit, when suddenly, a mighty fart breaks free from your arse like a thunderous explosion! The whole class turns to look at you, and you're left standing there like a proper bloody muppet, praying for a bloody escape route. But you know what? We've all been there, haven't we?

It's like yoga and bodily gases are bloody inseparable mates—always sneaking their way in, ready to steal the bloody show. And you know what? They don't give a flying f@ck. They're equal-opportunity embarrassers, targeting both the newbies and the seasoned yogis alike. So next time your butt decides to make a statement, just own that shite—figuratively and literally—and revel in the absolute absurdity of it all.

Burps, my good sods, burps are also the VIP guests of this f@cking yoga club of bodily surprises. You're deep in a peaceful pose, trying to find your inner tranquillity, when out of nowhere, a burp decides to make an appearance. It's like your stomach's performing a bloody burping concerto, and you can't help but wonder if the whole bloody class can hear it too.

But you know what, who the f@ck cares? Embrace these glorious bodily performances! They're just a reminder that we're all bloody human, and our bodies have their own unique ways of announcing their presence in this f@cking yoga extravaganza!

And you know what's even better? Sometimes, these little surprises can even spark a fit of laughter in the class. Imagine a f@cking domino effect of giggles and snorts rippling across the room like wildfire. It's like a secret comedy show right there on the yoga mats, with farts and burps as the f@cking headliners.

Fellow farting and burping experts, let's celebrate the hilarity of our bodies and their unpredictable performances. Let's revel in the f@cking laughter these noises bring, and let's remember that yoga is all about finding joy in the present moment, even if that moment involves a sweet impromptu farting solo.

And never bloody forget the golden rule of yoga class etiquette: if you let one rip, claim that shite! Flash a cheeky grin, blame it on the f@cking yoga mat if you must, and carry on like the yoga boss that you are.

Alright, you cheeky buggers, let's talk about how to avoid turning your yoga session into a fart and burp extravaganza! 'Cause let's be bloody honest, while those bodily noises can be a right laugh, we'd rather keep the symphony to a minimum, wouldn't we?

First things first, watch your bloody diet before you hit the yoga mat. I mean, you can't expect to have a peaceful yoga practice if you've loaded up on a feast of baked beans, cabbage, and onions beforehand. Your digestive system will be like a ticking time bomb, ready to unleash its gassy fury at the most inconvenient moment.

Here's a f@cking tip for you: go easy on the gas-producing foods before your class. Opt for some light, easily digestible fare that won't send your digestive system into overdrive. And for the love of all things holy, avoid the triple chilli burrito with extra hot sauce like it's the bloody plague.

And speaking of liquids, hydration is essential, but let's not go overboard and chug a gallon of water right before class. Trust me, you don't want to be that person frantically searching for the nearest bathroom mid-downward dog. It's like a f@cking Olympic event, trying to hold it in while striking your yoga poses. So, be smart and hydrate responsibly, my friends.

Oh, and here's a bloody tip for you: skip the fizzy drinks and sodas too. Those bubbly buggers can be a recipe for disaster, turning your yoga class into a burping bonanza. And nobody wants to be known as the "Yogi Burper," do they?

Now, let's talk timing. Give your digestive system some f@cking grace and allow it time to process your grub before you get your yoga on. Eating a three-course meal right before class is like asking for a fart symphony to accompany your practice. So, give it a good hour or two before you start stretching and contorting like a yoga god.

And here's a bonus tip: if you're feeling a bit bloated or gassy before class, don't be shy to let out a few gentle burps and farts before you begin. Get it out of your system like a boss, and then you can proceed with your practice feeling a bit more Zen and a lot less gassy.

Lastly, my fellow yogis, know your limits. If a certain pose or movement makes you feel like a human balloon ready to burst, back the f@ck off! Listen to your body, and if it's telling you to hold off on the deep twists and bends, bloody well listen to it.

Ok my gas-free yogis! Be mindful of what you eat before and after your practice, and you'll keep the yoga studio a blissful and gas-free zone. Remember, it's all about finding that balance on and off the mat, and avoiding the "gas chamber" scenarios will make everyone's yoga journey a lot more enjoyable. Now go forth and conquer that yoga mat like the gas-free warriors you are! Namaste and may your practice be filled with laughter, joy, and not a single accidental toot!

The mayhem Mat

Alright, brace yourselves for some annoying Mat Mayhem, my fellow yogi lunatics! This is where the yoga sh!t hits the fan and your peaceful practice turns into a full-blown comedy show.

All poised and ready to strike a fancy pose like a yoga master, but guess what? Your damn foot gets trapped in the strap of your yoga mat like it's auditioning for a role in a bloody comedy sketch!

Congratulations, you've just nailed the Mat Tango, a dance of frustration and hilarity. It's like your mat has developed a personality of its own and decided to play a f@cking prank on you. "Oh, you think you're gonna do that pose? Nah, mate, let's trip you up like a clumsy wanker on a banana peel!"

And if you manage to break free from the Mat Tango, hold on tight, 'cause here comes the Mat Twisty Twist. Your mat suddenly transforms into a demonic serpent, twisting and turning under your feet like it's possessed by the yoga gods of mischief.

You're left twisting and contorting like a f@cking human knot, wondering if you've accidentally stumbled into a circus act. The mat is probably cackling with glee as you struggle to maintain some semblance of balance.

But that's not all, my friends. The grand finale awaits: the f@cking face-plant! Yes, you heard that right. Just when you thought you've survived the Mat Tango and the Mat Twisty Twist, your mat decides to throw in one last surprise.

It rises up like a ninja from the depths of hell, tripping you up with its devious strap, and BAM! You find yourself sprawled on the ground, face-first, like a defeated warrior.

Oh, the spectacle it must be for your fellow yogis! But hey, don't fret. Embrace the chaos, laugh at the absurdity, and remember, it's all part of the bloody fun. Yoga isn't just about nailing those perfect poses; it's about finding joy in the hilarious mishaps along the way.

My fearless Mat Tango masters, go forth and conquer the Mat Mayhem. Twist, tangle, and tumble your way through the madness, and don't forget to enjoy the f@cking ride. Namaste, you crazy bunch of yoga lunatics!

Squeeky

Ah, behold the Human Squeak Toy, the star attraction in our very own yoga circus! Step right up, ladies and gents, and witness the wonders of yogis unintentionally transforming into a symphony of squeaky noises with every goddamn move they make. Move over sound effects, we've got ourselves a squeaky toy convention, and it's more entertaining than a comedy show!

Imagine a room filled with eager yogis trying to find their inner Zen, only to be greeted by a cacophony of squeaks and squawks that could rival a flock of squawking seagulls. It's a symphony of sound, my friends, a f@cking cacophony of squeakiness that'll have you questioning if you accidentally wandered into a f@cking pet store instead of a yoga studio!

As they move and contort their bodies, their joints emit the most delightful squeaky noises, as if they've been liberally doused in WD-40. Every stretch, every twist, and every bend is accompanied by a chorus of squeaks that could put a toy factory to shame.

It's like witnessing a tribe of squeaky aliens attempting to communicate through yoga poses, and let me tell you, it's a sight to behold. You'll have to fight back the urge to burst into laughter as the yoga class turns into a sideshow of hilarity.

And oh, the awkward glances and sheepish smiles as each yogi realizes they've become a human squeak toy! But fear not, my fellow yogis, for in this hilarious squeaky symphony, there is no judgment, only camaraderie in the shared experience of sounding like a bunch of f@cking rubber ducks.

Embrace the squeakiness, my friends. Let it be a reminder that yoga isn't always about silent serenity; sometimes, it's a raucous ride filled with unexpected surprises. And amidst the squeaks and squawks, find the joy and laughter that make yoga an adventure like no other.

And if you're lucky enough to have mastered the art of the Human Squeak Toy, wear that badge with pride. You're not just a yogi; you're a damn yoga entertainer, bringing smiles and laughter to all who have the pleasure of practising alongside you.

So, let the squeaky symphony play on, my fellow yogis. May your yoga sessions be filled with laughter, absurdity, and the delightful sound of the Human Squeak Toy in all its glory. Namaste, you hilarious bunch of squeaky legends!

Cramps

Oh, bloody hell! Can you believe it? Just when you're on the verge of becoming a friggin' yoga master, the universe decides to unleash the wrath of leg cramps upon you! It's like a cruel cosmic joke, testing your serenity in the most sadistic way possible.

Picture this nightmare: you're all Zen and centred, finding your inner peace, and then ZAK! A friggin' leg cramp hits you like a wrecking ball! It's like a fiery demon has possessed your limb, and you're left hopping around on one foot like a demented flamingo on acid.

And let me tell you, the pain is unreal! It's as if a herd of raging bulls has stampeded through your leg, trampling over every nerve and muscle in sight. You try to hold back the screams, but it's no use – the expletives just come pouring out, painting the yoga studio with a colourful array of curses.

But you know what? In the midst of this excruciating agony, you decide to channel your inner yogi badass. You turn that leg cramp into a friggin' yoga pose – behold, the Crampy Crab Asana! It's a damn miracle, my friends, a feat of human resilience that would put Hercules to shame.

As you hop around like a possessed jackrabbit, you catch the bewildered glances of your fellow yogis. They're either trying not to wet themselves with laughter or contemplating whether they should call for an exorcist. It's a sight to behold, a true carnival of chaos that would make Cirque du Soleil look like a kindergarten play.

And amidst all the mayhem, you start to wonder if the yoga gods are secretly punking you. "Oh, let's see how this poor soul handles a leg cramp in the middle of a damn yoga class," they must be saying, laughing their divine asses off.

But you know what, my fellow warriors of the yoga mat? You embrace the madness with open arms and rebel against the cramp with every fibre of your being. You turn that pain into a friggin' badge of honour, wearing it proudly like a battle scar.

The next time a leg cramp decides to gatecrash your Zen party, show it who's boss! Curse like a sailor, hop like a lunatic, and transform that damn cramp into the stuff of legends – the legendary Crampy Crab Asana, a testament to the indomitable spirit of the human soul.

And as you wobble through this bizarre dance of pain and hilarity, remember this – you're not alone. Every yogi has faced the wrath of the dreaded leg cramp, turning even the most composed guru into a cussing, hopping maniac.

So, my fellow Crampy Crabs, wear your leg cramps like a friggin' crown! Embrace the chaos, defy the universe with your resilience, and turn that godforsaken cramp into a dance of defiance. Namaste, you badass warriors of the yoga mat!

The wonderer

Oh, for fuck's sake, we've all encountered "The Wanderer" in the wild realm of yoga class. There's always that one lost soul, wandering around like a bewildered sheep, desperately searching for a fucking spot to plop their yoga mat. It's like they're on an expedition to find the bloody Holy Grail, when all they need is a little fucking patch of floor space.

You can't help but feel sorry for the poor bastard as they zigzag through the sea of yogis, looking like a lost tourist in a foreign fucking land. And what's their ultimate quest? Oh, it's the elusive spot, the sacred ground where their yoga journey will finally begin – or so they fucking believe.

But here's the thing, my fellow yogis – this ain't no grand adventure to uncover hidden treasures. It's yoga class! You can do this shit at home, for crying out loud! No need to embark on a goddamn pilgrimage through the sweaty bodies of your fellow practitioners.

As you watch "The Wanderer" in action, you can't help but stifle a fucking laugh. It's like they're auditioning for a role in a twisted yoga version of "The Amazing Race." If only there was a reality show called "Yoga Mat Hunt," they'd be the reigning champion.

And let's not forget their signature move – the awkward squat-and-scan manoeuvrer. You know the one I'm talking about – they crouch down like a deranged frog, scanning the floor with wide, desperate eyes, hoping for that magical fucking spot to reveal itself.

But alas, the stars are not aligned, and "The Wanderer" continues their odyssey. It's like they're on a perpetual quest to find the holy grail of yoga class locations. The irony is, there are empty spaces all around them, but they remain fucking blind to the possibilities.

Dear "Wandering Yogi," let me offer you a piece of advice – calm the fuck down! Take a deep breath, pick a spot, any damn spot, and claim it as your own. It's not rocket science; it's just friggin' yoga!

But who am I to fucking judge? We've all been there – lost, confused, and feeling like a moron in the pursuit of the perfect yoga spot. So let's raise a glass to "The Wanderer," the brave soul who dares to navigate the treacherous terrain of the yoga class floor.

If you ever find yourself on a similar quest, just remember – you're not alone in this hilarious pilgrimage. Embrace the wandering spirit within, turn it into a new yoga style, and may the fucking yoga gods guide you to your spot of serenity.

Let the Wandering Yogi Flow be your fucking signature move. Embrace the chaos, embrace the laughter, and remember, my dear lost soul – the journey is just as fun as the destination. Namaste, you glorious nomads of the yoga mat!

Chapter 15

YOGA OFF MAT

Alright, brace yourselves fer the bloody nutters who've taken the concept o' yoga and turned it into a proper circus show! We're diving into the weirdest places where these mad bastards decide it's a grand idea to do their bendy nonsense, so don't say I did not warn you! And mind you, if ye get yourself in trouble, don't come cryin' to me!

Yoga on a Roller Coaster: Strap yourself in and hold on tight, 'cause these daft wankers are doing yoga on a bloody roller coaster! Imagine trying to do a Warrior Pose while the coaster's twisting and turning. I mean, you're supposed to be enjoying the thrill, no trying to channel your inner yogi!

Yoga in a Busy Subway: In the middle of rush hour, these idiots think it's a brilliant idea to do their tree poses and whatnot in a crowded subway wagon. Personal space? Forget about it! Embrace the sweaty armpits and elbow jabs as ye struggle to find their inner calm.

Yoga in the Supermarket: Picture yourself reaching for a box of cereal, and there's some pillock doing a Standing Forward Fold right next to you. I mean, who needs peace and quiet while grocery shopping, right? Pure madness, I tell you.

Yoga in a Laundromat: Hey, why not do a bit o' yoga while ye wait for your laundry? Imagine doing poses amidst the hum o' washing machines and the scent o' detergent. People will be thinking, "Is this wanker for real?"

Yoga on a Paddle-board: Doing yoga on a wobbly paddle-board? Are ye taking the piss? I'd pay good money to see these numpties trying tae do a headstand and end up in the water. Talk about a good laugh!

Yoga in an Elevator: In a cramped elevator with strangers, they're doing yoga poses like it's a bleeding studio. As if the ride's no already uncomfortable enough! Who needs peace when ye can have awkward glances and muffled laughter?

7. Yoga at a Busy Intersection: Doing yoga in the middle of a traffic jam. Picture yourself striking a Warrior Pose as cars honk and folks gawk. If ye want to get run over, go right ahead!

Yoga in a Movie Theatre: Bored during the previews? Time to entertain yourself and annoy everyone else with some stealthy yoga moves. Imagine doing a Crow Pose during an action scene. You'll be the star o' the show, for sure!

Yoga at the Airport Security Check: Doing yoga while waiting in line fer airport security? Are ye mental? Imagine doing stretches and breathing exercises as folks around ye grumble and curse. Talk about attention-seeking'!

Yoga in a Haunted House: Picture yourself doing yoga amidst creaks and ghostly moans. I'm telling ya, you'll have the bloody spirits joining in on the fun. Good luck explaining that one!

Yoga at the DMV: What? Doing yoga while waiting at the Department of Motor Vehicles? Imagine their Zen nonsense amidst folks losing their minds. You'll be the one stickin' out like a sore thumb, and not in a good way.

Yoga at a Petting Zoo: Doing yoga amidst adorable animals. You are doing a Cat Pose while actual cats wander 'round? You are gonna end up covered in fur and goat shit!

Yoga in a Buffet: Aye, mindful eating at a buffet. Are ye off your mind? You're surrounded by food, and you decide to do yoga? A buffet is fer eating, not stretching!

Yoga at Sunday Mass: Picture yourself doing yoga during a full Sunday Mass in a church. Pure blasphemy! The priest will be giving you a proper bollocking, and rightfully so.

Yoga at a Funeral: OK, picture yourself doing yoga next to a casket. The deceased might've been a yoga master, but that doesn't mean ye should imitate 'em! It's a funeral, not a f@cking morbid yoga studio.

Yoga at the Doctor's Office: while waiting for your appointment, and some daft bugger's decided it's a perfect time to do a Downward Dog. As if ye don't have enough to worry about already!

19. Yoga at the Dentist: of course, just imagine doing a Tree Pose while the dentist's got his fingers in your gob. Dental work is torture enough without adding yoga to the mix.

Yoga during a Massage: You're supposed to relax during a massage, not doing a Sun Salutation! These loonies cannae resist the urge to stretch even when they're getting pampered.

Yoga in the Bedroom: Making love with a partner is meant to be intimate and passionate, but now they've got these yogi weirdos doing poses mid-shag. I mean, ye cannot make this shite up!

Yoga at a Business Meeting: yes, why not do a bit o' chair yoga during a meeting? It'll surely impress the boss, especially when ye accidentally knock o'er the coffee with your flailing arms.

Yoga at the Disco while Drunk: that's actually might be cool! Imagine being sloshed at a disco and doing yoga on the dance floor. You'd be lucky if don't trip over!

Yoga in the Middle of a Riot: In the midst o' chaos and protests, these morons think it's the perfect time to do their inner peace sh!t. Trust me, nobody's paying attention to your Warrior Pose when there's tear gas in the air.

Yoga on a Moving Train: In the middle of a packed train, these daft w@nkers decide to strike a pose. It's like watching a contortionist perform in a sardine can. I mean, have they no shame?

Yoga at a Police Station: While waiting to get bailed out, some pillock thinks it's a grand idea to do a bit o' yoga. It's a police station, not a wellness retreat!

Yoga at a Comedy Show: Picture yourself doing yoga poses in the middle of a comedy show. You'll be the punchline, that's for sure!

Yoga at the Tattoo Parlour: while gettin' inked, and some nutter thinks it's a perfect time to do yoga. I mean, you are trying to stay still for the artist, not doing a bloody yoga flow!

Yoga at the Pub: Imagine doing yoga at the local pub while everyone's getting plastered. You'll be the entertainment for the night, not a sh!t depressing pub no more!

Yoga at a Dog Park: Imagine trying to do yoga while dogs are barking and running all around ye. There'll be dodging' doggy paws and poop while you trying to maintain your "Zen" Good luck with that!

Yoga at the Library: you are supposed to be quiet in a library, but now these nutters are doing yoga between the bookshelves. Shhh, indeed! The librarian will be chasin' 'em out with a "Keep Quiet" sign!

Yoga in a Haunted House: It's Halloween, and these daft buggers think it's a brilliant idea to do yoga in a haunted house. They'll be screamin' louder than any ghost when they feel a tap on their shoulder during Savasana!

Yoga in the Middle of a Street Parade: Among the floats and dancers, there they are, doing yoga poses in the middle o' a street parade. The crowd's cheering fer the parade, but they'll be cheering even louder fer these daft yogis!

Yoga in the Middle of a Food Court: Amidst the smell o' fast food, these nutters are doing yoga on the floor of a busy food court. It's a feast fer the senses, but no one's ordering what they're selling!

Yoga in a Police Line-up: Picture yourself doing yoga poses while standing in a line-up with actual criminals. The coppers will think they've got a right circus on their hands!

Yoga in a Cemetery: It's a graveyard, not a f@cking yoga retreat! But there they are, doing poses next to tombstones. They'll be communicating with the spirits if they're no careful!

Yoga in a Nightclub Queue: while you are waiting to get into a nightclub, and these daft buggers think it's a grand idea to do some yoga while they wait. They'll be in a different kind o' queue if they don't watch out!

Yoga in the Middle of a Soccer Match: As everyone's cheering fer their team, these ninnies are doing yoga poses on the sidelines. The players will be wondering if they've stumbled into a parallel universe!

A bunch of proper mental nutters doing yoga in the weirdest places. If you wanna embarrass yourself and end up in some awkward situations, go ahead, knock yourself out. But don't say I didn't warn you! These daft buggers have taken yoga to a whole new level of madness. If ye've got the cojones for it, go ahead and embrace the insanity, it might be fun!

Chapter 16

WEIRD PLACES AND SITUATIONS

When yoga and mindfulness decide to tango, it's like watching a two-left-footed couple attempting ballroom dance – the serenity of inner peace meets the hilarious havoc of cosmic confusion, resulting in a befuddled brouhaha that leaves both practices wondering if they accidentally stepped on each other's toes during their clumsy choreography. In the previous chapter I listed few but here we are on another level…

Yoga in the park

Alright, listen up, you lot! You know those characters you come across in the park on a peaceful Sunday morning? Yeah, the ones moving like they've had a dodgy date with magic mushrooms in their salad and chugged a pint of Valium. Taichi, they call it, but it looks more like interpretive dance from another dimension! And then there's the so-called "pranayama pros" glowing like bloody gods, attempting to find Zen amidst the chaos of the park. I mean, hats off to 'em, but how the bloody hell do they focus with dogs barking, tramps shouting, and birds squawking like they swallowed a bloody megaphone?

I'll tell you what, I absolutely love 'em! They've got the patience of saints, or maybe they've mastered the art of selective hearing. I mean, if it were me, I'd lose my cool faster than a cheetah chasing its prey. Picture this: a yogi, all Zen and composed, trying to find inner peace while a bird's massive shit splatters right on their head. Oh, the irony!

But you know what? They're not giving up that easily. They power through, undeterred by the madness around 'em, like they've got some secret superpower to block out the chaos. It's like watching a real-life superhero, cape and all, taking on the park's cacophony with nothing but their serenity to protect 'em.

And the occasional mishaps? Sometimes, in their quest for inner peace, they end up tangled in their own limbs, looking like a pretzel that's been through a blender. But hey, they laugh it off, and that's what I admire about 'em. They don't take themselves too seriously, even when they look like a contorted mess.

You know what's the best part? After all the yoga and Zen, they've earned themselves a bloody pint! Oh yes, they head straight to the pub, ready to down a cold one and say "Cheers!" to a morning of enlightenment, chaos, and bird sh!t. And you know what? I'll raise my glass to 'em too, 'cause they've got the spirit, the tenacity, and the sense of humor to tackle life's absurdity with grace.

So here's to the park yogis, the Taichi dancers, and the pranayama pros—the brave souls navigating the unpredictable circus of life and finding their inner calm amidst the madness. Cheers to their resilience, their patience, and their ability to keep their cool even when the world around 'em goes bonkers. Here's to the warriors of peace, the laughter amid chaos, and the pint that caps off a morning of yoga and absolute bloody mayhem! Cheers, my friends, and may your yoga practice be as wild and wonderful as the park itself!

Yoga office

Alright, brace yourselves for the cringe-worthy tale of the "Office Yogi" gone wild!

So, picture this, you're slogging through your workday, trying to get shit done, and there's this Zen colleague of yours who thinks they're the reincarnation of some Indian god on a cosmic bender. Instead of just stretching a bit during the day like a normal human, they decide to bring the feckin' yoga studio to the office!

They start by striking a pose in the middle of the cubicles, like they're auditioning for a yoga-themed episode of "The Office." Downward facing dog? More like downward facing d!ckhead, if you ask me! And there they go, talking to their arse as if it's the Dalai Lama's long-lost cousin.

The boss walks by, raises an eyebrow, and asks, "What the bloody hell are you doing?" And what do they say? Oh, get ready for this, my friends! They put on this fake-ass Indian accent, sounding like a bad Bollywood movie on steroids, and say, "I am channelling the ancient wisdom of the yogis to harmonize my chakras and awaken my inner Shiva." S

You can feel the second-hand embarrassment oozing out of every pore in the room. It's like a bad karaoke performance mixed with a terrible stand-up routine. You'd think they were auditioning for a role in a Shakespearean comedy—only this is an office, not the Globe Theatre!

But they don't stop there. Oh no, they go full-on Shakespearean drama mode, adding in some weird-ass mudras and chants. It's like they're summoning spirits or trying to put a curse on the photocopier. I mean, it's okay to do some stretching, but this is some next-level bullsh!t right here!

The whole office is trying to keep a straight face, but inside, we're all dying with laughter. It's like a scene from a cringe-worthy sitcom that you can't look away from. And just when you think it can't get any worse, they start preaching about the benefits of yoga like some enlightened guru.

"You see, my dear colleagues," they say, with a hint of superiority in their voice, "yoga is the path to eternal bliss and divine enlightenment. You must connect with the cosmic energy and let the universe flow through you like a river of blissful tranquillity."

Meanwhile, the rest of us are thinking, "Yeah, mate, we'll take that cosmic energy and flow it straight out the window if you don't shut the f@ck up!"

But here's the kicker—they're completely oblivious to how ridiculous they look and sound. They're lost in their own little yogi bubble, floating on a cloud of delusion, while the rest of us are trying not to burst out laughing in their face.

In the end, we all just nod politely, like we're listening to a madman's ramblings, and go back to our work. But you can bet your arse that the office legend of the "Office Yogi" is born, and we'll be swapping stories about this yoga-talking-to-the-arse guru for years to come.

So, there you have it, the cringiest, most embarrassing office moment of all time. And we thought office politics were bad! Who knew yoga could turn an ordinary workplace into a full-blown circus of lunacy? Namaste my arse!

The zen parents

Ah, the frustrations of the "Zen parents" trying to achieve nirvana with their little rascals! Picture this, the parents attempting to meditate for just two minutes, only to be interrupted every five seconds with cries for snacks, toys, and every f@cking thing under the sun. "Sit down for two minutes, mammy just needs a moment of peace, and I'll give you a bloody ice cream!"

But do the kids give a flying f@ck about inner peace? Absolutely not! They see their Zen-seeking parents as walking vending machines, and they won't settle for anything less than instant gratification. "Mummy, I want that toy now! Gimme, gimme, gimme!"

The parents resort to desperate measures to buy themselves some peace. "Alright, kiddo, sit still for two minutes, and I'll get you that shiny new toy you've been eyeing for weeks. Please, just shut the f@ck up for a minute!"

But let's be real, achieving Zen in the presence of these miniature dictators is like searching for a f@cking unicorn. Every time they manage to sit down, the kids unleash a torrent of demands and complaints, leaving the parents in a constant state of frustration. "Meditate? More like med-irritate! These bloody little buggers are driving me insane!"

The parents start to wonder if they'll ever find a moment of peace again. "Maybe if I lock myself in the bathroom and pretend to be taking a sh!t, they'll leave me alone for a minute!"

Alas, there's no escape from the tiny tyrants. They follow the parents everywhere, demanding attention and snacks and more f@cking snacks. "Mummy, I want chocolate! I want chips! I want a f@cking unicorn!"

The parents try to find solace in the chaos, telling themselves that it's all just part of the parenting journey. "One day, they'll grow up, and I'll finally get to meditate in peace. Until then, I'll just have to meditate with my eyes open, ready to deal with whatever sh!tstorm they throw my way."

And so, the quest for zen continues, amidst the tantrums, the demands, and the constant interruptions. "Meditation? More like medit-f@cking-ation! These little buggers won't let me have a moment's peace!"

But hey, amidst the frustrations and the chaos, there are moments of love and joy that make it all worthwhile. "They may drive me up the f@cking wall, but I wouldn't trade them for anything in the world. Even if they do make meditation feel like a f@cking pipe dream!"

A.S.Salomone

Traffic

Ah, the "yoga in the traffic jam" enthusiasts. You know the type - stuck in a gridlock of cars, but instead of trying to find a way out, they decide to strike a pose on the side of the road like it's some kind of serene yoga studio. "Ohm, ohm, ohm, let me find my inner peace while the honking horns and exhaust fumes surround me!"

Picture this: there they are, standing outside their cars, attempting to do a bloody tree pose as the rest of us are losing our minds and turning into Michael Douglas from "Falling Down." But no, they're not bothered by the chaos around them because they're too busy finding their Zen, or at least pretending to.

Meanwhile, the rest of us are sitting in our cars, glaring at these "yoga in the traffic jam" morons, wondering why they can't just sit down and stop holding up the traffic even more. "Oh look, darling, it's the enlightened yogis causing the hold-up this time. Brilliant!"

But they're not just content with doing tree poses. Oh no, they have to take it up a notch and start doing sun salutations on the side-walk. "Namaste, fellow drivers, I'll be doing my sun salutations here, just ignore me while I block your way!"

What about the ones who decide to do some deep breathing exercises right in the middle of the road.? "Just breathe, everyone, it's not like we're in a hurry to get anywhere!"

But here's the thing, "yoga in the traffic jam" crew - your enlightened poses won't make the traffic magically disappear. "Ohm, ohm, ohm, I'm channelling my inner traffic controller to clear the roads!"

No, all you're doing is making us want to scream and pull our hair out. "For f@ck's sake, just get back in your car and drive like the rest of us!"

So, to all you aspiring traffic jam yogis, do us all a favor and keep your yoga poses to yourself. "Ohm, ohm, ohm, I promise not to do yoga in the traffic jam ever again. Now please, just let me merge into the lane!"

Cooking

Oh, here we go, the "yoga chef" brigade, thinking they can find mindfulness while cooking! Like, seriously, who comes up with this sh!t? They believe that by striking a pose while chopping onions, their dishes will magically taste better. I mean, come on, it's not like the onions are going to start crying tears of joy because you're doing a downward facing dog!

Picture this, the "yoga chef" in their pristine kitchen, wearing their fancy apron and trying to balance on one leg while stirring the pot. It's like a bloody circus act in there! "Look at me, I'm a culinary yogi, bringing inner peace to my spaghetti bolognese!"

But let's be real, no amount of yoga poses is going to turn your burnt toast into a gourmet meal. "Ohm, ohm, ohm, I'm chanting for the burnt bits to magically disappear!"

And don't get me started on their so-called "mindful eating." They take one tiny bite of their avocado toast and spend the next five minutes savouring it like it's the most profound experience of their lives. "Mmm, I can taste the universe in this avocado!"

Meanwhile, the rest of us are just trying to eat our breakfast without choking on our laughter. "Mindful eating? More like mind-numbing eating! Just bloody eat the avocado and get on with it!"

But the "yoga chefs" are relentless. They believe that every step of the cooking process must be done with utmost mindfulness and intention. "I'm going to breathe deeply while I boil water for pasta. Maybe it will make it cook faster!"

And let's not forget their obsession with organic, gluten-free, cruelty-free, vegan, non-GMO, fair-trade ingredients. "My food is so pure and virtuous, it practically levitates off the plate!"

But guess what, "yoga chefs"? Your pretentious ingredients won't save you from burning the f@ck out of your quinoa. "Oh no, I overcooked the quinoa! Maybe if I do a sun salutation, it will magically unburnt!"

In the end, all their mindfulness and yoga poses can't hide the fact that their food tastes like bland cardboard. "Congratulations, you've mastered the art of tasteless cooking!"

So, to all you aspiring "yoga chefs" out there, save your downward dogs for the yoga mat and leave the cooking to the professionals. NamasTea and buon appetito (or whatever the f@ck).

Mindful washing up

Ah, the "mindful mishap" crew, trying to apply mindfulness to the most mundane tasks like washing dishes. Because apparently, if you wash those dishes with enough presence and serenity, all your problems will vanish like the bloody bubbles in the sink. "Ohm, ohm, ohm, I'll wash these dishes with such mindfulness that my student loan debt will magically disappear!"

So there you are, standing at the sink, scrubbing away like a Zen master, contemplating the meaning of life while the dirty dishes pile up around you. "Ohm, ohm, ohm, I am one with the dishes, and the dishes are one with me. Just don't mind the mouldy cheese that's been stuck on this plate for days."

But let's be real for a moment - no amount of mindfulness is going to make that crusty lasagna dish easier to clean. "Ohm, ohm, ohm, maybe if I breathe deeply enough, the lasagna will magically wash itself."

And as you stand there, lost in your thoughts, your mind starts to wander to all the other things you could be doing instead. "Ohm, ohm, ohm, I could be binge-watching Netflix right now, but no, I'm stuck here in the mindfulness prison of washing dishes."

But of course, you can't just stop at washing dishes. Oh no, you have to apply mindfulness to everything you do, even taking out the trash. "Ohm, ohm, ohm, I'll take out the trash with such mindfulness that I'll become one with the garbage."

The ultimate test of mindfulness - dealing with a clogged drain. "Ohm, ohm, ohm, maybe if I stare at the drain long enough, it will unclog itself. Or better yet, maybe I can meditate the clog away!"

But here's the reality, "mindful mishap" crew - life is messy, and no amount of mindfulness is going to change that. "Ohm, ohm, ohm, I am one with the mess. Screw it, I'm hiring a cleaning service."

Dear folks—the mind-boggling madness of turning everyday tasks into a spiritual circus. Because apparently, life's not complicated enough, and we all need a healthy dose of cosmic craziness to make it through. So go ahead, channel your inner Yogi McMindfulpants as you wash dishes, deal with traffic, parent your offspring, and burn your dinner. It's like living in a kaleidoscope of chaos and enlightenment all rolled into one.

So, to all you aspiring mindfulness gurus, here's a tip: it's okay to let go of the mindfulness act and embrace the chaos of life. "Ohm, ohm, ohm, I'm done with this mindfulness nonsense. Time for a pint and some real relaxation."

Cheers to that!

Chapter 17

INCREDIBLY CRAZY YOGA CLASSES!

Let me tell ya about these bloody mental yoga classes that have taken the world by storm. I mean, seriously, have you seen this f@cking list, my dear BnB pals? It's like they're trying to see just how far they can push the boundaries of human sanity with this bollocks

All these yoga classes EXIST!!! It's not my twisted mind my friends!

First off, we got yoga with creepy dolls. Are you kiddin' me? Who in their right mind wants to do the downward dog next to a ruddy doll that looks like it crawled out of a horror flick? It's enough to give ya the bloody creeps.

And hold on to your knickers, 'cause it gets even more bonkers! How 'bout yoga on a hot air balloon? Oh, sure, let's try to find inner peace while we're floating hundreds of feet above the ground. 'Cause that's not terrifying at all!

But wait, there's more! Buckle up for yoga on icebergs. Yeah, 'cause what better way to connect with your inner self than by freezing your arse off in icy waters? I swear, these folks must be off their rockers.

If that's not enough to make ya question humanity, get this – yoga in haunted houses. Oh, great! Let's try to find our Zen while dodging spooky spirits and things that go bump in the night. 'Cause that sounds relaxing, doesn't it?

And just when you think it can't get any more barmy, they hit ya with yoga on horseback. I mean, seriously, who dreams up this shite? "Oh, just balance on a ruddy horse while doing a Tree Pose!" Yeah, right, I'll pass on that one, thanks.

But you know what, my fellow BnB, as daft as all this sounds, there's somethin' oddly entertaining about it. I mean, who wouldn't wanna try yoga on a ruddy helipad with the whole city spread out before ya? It's like being in your own action movie, minus all the explosions.

So, if you're up for a laugh and a bit of a mad adventure, go ahead and give one of these bloody mental yoga classes a go. It might just be the most bonkers thing you've ever done, but hey, at least you'll have a story to tell at the pub.

The mighty list:

1. Goat Yoga: Because nothing says "serenity now" like having a bunch of bleating goats hopping all over you. Namaste, my furry little friends.

2. Naked Yoga: Who needs clothes when you can let it all hang out and find your inner yogi exhibitionist? Just hope there are no downward-facing cameras.

3. Disco Yoga: Get ready to "Stayin' Alive" in the most fabulous and groovy yoga class ever. Bring your best dance moves and your brightest spandex.

4. Cat Yoga: Because balancing in a pose is so much easier when there's a feline trying to knock you off your feet. Namaste, you little devils.

5. Aerial Yoga: Who needs solid ground when you can float like a majestic yoga wizard? Just don't forget to bring your magic broomstick.

6. Laughter Yoga: Because life's too short to take yoga seriously. Chuckle your way to enlightenment, folks.

7. Doga: Because why do yoga alone when you can do it with your canine BFF? Just be prepared for some curious sniffing during your practice.

8. Beer Yoga: When you want to combine relaxation with a boozy buzz, this one's for you. Cheers to tipsy balance and wobbly poses.

9. Karaoke Yoga: It's like American Idol and yoga had a weird, hilarious baby. Strike a pose, belt out a tune, and hope Simon Cowell doesn't show up.

10. Blindfolded Yoga: Because nothing says "zen" like stumbling around in the dark and hoping you don't accidentally kick someone. Find your inner yogi daredevil.

11. Stand-Up Paddleboard Yoga: Because why settle for solid ground when you can risk falling into the icy depths of the water? It's like playing Twister on a floating plank of doom.

12. Metal Yoga: Prepare to headbang your way to inner peace, because nothing says "zen" like deafening guitar riffs and guttural screams. Namaste, motherf@~kers.

13. Glow-in-the-Dark Yoga: Get ready to flow in a neon-lit rave cave, because who needs natural light when you can contort yourself in psychedelic glow?

14. Yoga hippy Rock: It's like Woodstock meets a downward dog. Let the pulsating beats lead you to enlightenment, and try not to trip over the flowers power friends.

15. Underwater Yoga: Dive deep into the abyss of your practice, where breathing becomes a daring challenge and drowning is just an inconvenient possibility.

16. Chocolate Yoga: Because when you think yoga, you naturally think of stuffing your face with chocolate. It's the ultimate indulgence for your sweet tooth and your downward-facing cravings.

17. Inflatable Yoga: It's like doing yoga on a bouncy castle, because who doesn't want to add a dash of whimsy to their practice? Just don't get carried away and accidentally float away to Neverland.

18. Harry Potter Yoga: Prepare to cast spells and strike poses as you journey to the wizarding world of yoga. Accio inner peace!

19. Drag Queen Yoga: Werk it, honey! Let the fabulous queens guide you through a yoga practice that's sassy, fierce, and sprinkled with glitter.

20. Yoga Alpacas: Because when you think of yoga, you naturally think of fluffy farm animals. Downward dog becomes downward goat, and shavasana turns into a snuggle fest with alpacas. Just don't let the alpacas eat your yoga pants.

21. Trampoline Yoga: Because bouncing like a maniac on a trampoline totally enhances your inner peace. It's like trying to find zen while being a human pogo stick.

22. Yoga with Baby Animals: Because what's more calming than being surrounded by adorable baby critters? Just try not to get distracted by their cuteness and fall flat on your face.

23. Silent Disco Yoga: It's like a solo dance party meets yoga class. Flow through your practice in silence, except for the occasional yogi breaking out into an off-key hum.

24. Circus Yoga: Roll up, roll up for the greatest show on earth! It's like being in a three-ring circus, except instead of lions and trapeze artists, you've got yogis attempting acrobatics.

25. Skateboard Yoga: Take your practice from the mat to the halfpipe, because nothing says inner peace like risking a broken ankle while attempting a handstand on a skateboard.

26. Yoga in a Salt Cave: Because salty air and downward dog are the perfect combo for enlightenment. Just make sure you don't accidentally lick the walls during your practice.

27. Rooftop Yoga: Rise above the city noise and find your inner calm while dodging pigeon droppings on the rooftop. It's like urban yoga with a side of aerial pigeon watching.

28. Yoga with Wine Tasting: Because why not combine two great things: yoga and getting sloshed. Flow through poses with a wine glass in hand, just don't let the instructor catch you trying to balance a bottle on your head.

29. Glowga: It's like a rave party meets a yoga class. Get your glow on and flow through poses in the neon lights. Just try not to bump into your fellow glowga yogis.

30. Yoga in a Haunted House: Embrace the spooky vibes and find your inner peace while being surrounded by creaky floors and creepy ghosts. Don't be surprised if your chakras start tingling with fear.

31. Yoga with Baby Dolls: Because nothing says "finding your zen" like cradling creepy baby dolls while attempting a sun salutation. Try not to let the dolls stare into your soul during shavasana.

32. Yoga with Virtual Reality: Why settle for the real world when you can escape into a virtual one? Flow through poses while pretending you're a warrior in a fantasy realm. Just make sure not to trip over real-world obstacles.

33. Yoga in a Labyrinth: It's like trying to find inner peace while being lost in a maze. Flow through poses while navigating twists and turns, and try not to get stuck in a downward dog dead-end.

34. Yoga in the Dark: Because trying to balance in a dark room with zero visibility totally enhances your yoga experience. It's like yoga blindfolded, but without the blindfold.

35. Yoga in the Clouds: Elevate your practice to new heights by floating in a hot air balloon. Because nothing says "finding your centre" like attempting yoga poses while praying not to plummet back to earth.

36. Ice Yoga: Because nothing says inner peace like freezing your asana off on a frigid ice rink. It's like trying to find balance while your toes turn into icicles.

37. Yoga with Puppies: Because what's more zen than being trampled by a herd of adorable puppies? Just try not to get distracted by their playful antics while attempting a peaceful pose.

38. Yoga in a Treehouse: Channel your inner monkey as you attempt to find your center in a rickety treehouse. It's like trying to be a yogi while playing a real-life game of "Don't Look Down."

39. Yoga in the Rainforest: Let the soothing sounds of nature lull you into a false sense of serenity while you try not to trip over tree roots and fend off mosquitos.

40. Yoga in the Desert: Because doing yoga on a sandy surface with scorching heat is totally the key to enlightenment. Just don't forget to bring plenty of water and sunscreen for your sweaty, sun-baked practice. Sauna yoga new level!

41. Yoga with Live Music: Nothing like trying to find your inner peace while dodging flying drumsticks and guitar picks. It's like a rock concert meets a yoga class, minus the mosh pit.

42. Yoga on Horseback: Get ready to saddle up and attempt yoga poses on a moving horse. It's like being in a bucking bronco rodeo, but with more downward dogs.

43. Yoga in a Laundrymat: While waiting your clothes to be ready, why don't you do a warrior 2? Oh yeas I can now! And my chakras are spinning at the same time washing machine!

44. Yoga in a Hot Spring: Because nothing says tranquility like trying to find your center in a steamy, crowded hot spring. It's like being in a human stew of floating yogis.

45. Yoga in a Vineyard: Flow through poses in between sips of wine, because nothing says "namaste" like being tipsy on the mat. Just try not to confuse your vinyasa with your Merlot.

46. Yoga on Icebergs: It's like trying to find inner peace while teetering on the edge of a frozen abyss. One wrong move, and you'll be doing an unintentional polar plunge.

47. Yoga with Martial Arts: Because why settle for one physical discipline when you can combine two and risk looking like a flailing ninja trying to meditate.

48. Yoga on a Helipad: Elevate your practice to new heights and hope that a sudden gust of wind doesn't elevate you even higher. It's like doing yoga in the clouds, with a side of vertigo.

49. Yoga with Fire Dancing: Attempt yoga poses while fire dancers twirl and spin around you. It's like trying to find your inner peace while surrounded by a fiery circus.

50. Yoga in a Sunflower Field: Because nothing says serenity like practising yoga while bees buzz around and sunflowers tower over you. It's like being in a nature-themed obstacle course of beauty and chaos.

51. Wine yoga: Best class ever. The hangover? Zen-tastic!

52. yoga raves: It doesn't make sense at all! I mean, I've been if few raves and I was as fast as Flash on cocaine! How that hell can do that class?

53. Cannabis yoga: Ya man! It must be the most Zen class ever! Rastavasana!

54. Tantrum yoga: Why not? I'ts sound so f@cked up that I would try it!

55. Broga Yoga: Broga is the trademarked type of yoga class specifically marketed to men and athletically inclined individuals that believe they do not have the flexibility for other yoga classes! Yes Men are stupid.

Seriously, folks, what on earth is going on? These yoga classes are absolutely mind-boggling. I can't help but wonder if there are even more ridiculously bizarre things out there, but this list alone should give you a taste of just how strange our world can be. Personally, I'll stick to my yoga exercises, but my friend is having a blast exploring more of these peculiarities. Remember to stay safe and enjoy the journey!

NamasTea!

Chapter 18

INTO THE WILD

Alright, buckle up, you lot, 'cause we're diving head first into the wild world of nature-loving yogis. Picture this, a bunch of blokes and birds, all decked out in their fancy yoga gear, thinking they've become one with Mother Nature just because they're doing a bloody downward dog on a patch of grass. Oh, the hilarity that f@cking ensues!

First off, you've got your Zen-zillas attempting the tree pose like they're auditioning for a f@cking role in "Tarzan: The Musical." They flail their arms and legs like they're being chased by a swarm of wasps, and, God forbid, a breeze comes by, and they're all over the place like leaves in a f@cking hurricane. It's a right tree-tastrophe!

Then, there's the fearless lot, thinking they can impress the animal kingdom with their fearless poses. They've got the bollocks to strike a cobra pose right in front of a bunch of real cobras. I mean, are they mad or just plain dim? One wrong move, and they'll be joining Steve Irwin in the afterlife. f@cking crikey!

And let's not forget the "hippie-dippie-wildlife whisperers." They're convinced they can telepathically communicate with the woodland critters. They attempt to do the pigeon pose, hoping to attract actual pigeons, but all they get are squirrels laughing their furry tails off. Talk about a f@cking squirrelly showdown!

But the pièce de résistance, my dear readers, is the "Yogi Bear" brigade. These wankers attempt to do bear poses right in the heart of bear territory. I mean, what's the plan here? Do they think they'll commune with the bears and share a spot of tea? More like a f@cking spot of being someone's lunch! It's a bear-nado waiting to happen!

And don't even get me started on the brave souls trying the fish pose right next to a river full of actual f@cking fish. They end up getting more attention from seagulls than fish. It's like a fish market in the sky, with the birds circling and squawking like they've hit the f@cking jackpot.

Oh, The serene meditators, closing their eyes and trying to be one with the universe while surrounded by buzzing mosquitoes and dive-bombing bees. I don't know about you, but I'd rather be at home with a cuppa than meditating in a swarm of bloodthirsty insects.

Here, you daft buggers, a right natural circus of yoga gone f@cking wild. These nature-loving yogis may think they're one with the wilderness, but they're more like a bunch of animals on a safari gone wrong. It's a comedy of f@cking errors, a disaster waiting to happen, and I must say, it's a right laugh to watch.

And just remember, next time you're tempted to strike a pose in the great outdoors, beware of the wild wonders that f f@cking await. Stay safe, stay sane, and for the love of all things holy, avoid trying to commune with the local wildlife. Namaste, my fellow adventurers, and may your yoga in nature be more comedy than f@cking catastrophe!

Now, as much as I've taken the piss out of these nature-loving yogis, I must admit there's something oddly endearing about their antics. You can't help but admire their spirit and determination, even if it's mixed with a good dose of delusion. And let's be honest, we could all use a bit of that wild optimism in our lives.

I mean, who wouldn't want to believe that doing yoga in the great outdoors will make them one with the universe? It's a bit like hoping that eating a kale salad will magically turn you into a freaky superhuman. We all know it's bollocks, but it's fun to dream, innit?

And I must say, there's something strangely liberating about doing yoga in nature. Sure, you might look like a prat, but who gives a toss? You're out there, breathing in the fresh air, feeling the sun on your skin, and giving zero fucks about what anyone else thinks. It's like a rebellious act of self-care, a big middle finger to the constraints of modern life.

So, while these nature-loving yogis might be a right laugh to watch, there's something admirable about their willingness to embrace the wild side of life. They remind us that it's okay to be a bit daft, to let go of our inhibitions, and to find joy in the most unexpected places.

And who knows, maybe there's some truth to their belief that nature and yoga can bring us closer to something greater than ourselves. Maybe, just maybe, in those moments of peace and stillness, we do feel a connection to the world around us, a sense of belonging to something larger than our own little bubble.

To all you adventurous yogis out there, keep doing your thing in nature, even if it makes you look like a right nutter. Embrace the chaos, the laughter, and the occasional swarm of mosquitoes. It's all part of the wild ride that is yoga in the great outdoors.

For the rest of us, let's not be too quick to judge. Instead, let's find inspiration in their wild spirit and remember that sometimes, it's okay to let go, to be a bit bonkers, and to find our own little slice of Zen in the midst of nature's madness.

NamasTea, you glorious bunch of nature-loving nutters.

May your yoga adventures continue to be full of laughter, surprises, and a healthy dose of f@cking charm. Cheers to finding peace and hilarity in the great outdoors!

Just in case you're not quite sold on the whole "yoga in nature" gig but still fancy getting your Zen on without looking like a daft bugger, fear not! I've got some fun alternatives for you to consider:

"Urban Yoga Warrior": Embrace the concrete jungle as your playground. Strike your best warrior pose while waiting for the bus, do a quick downward dog at the office during your coffee break, or attempt a tree pose on a park bench. Just be prepared for some odd looks from passers-by - but who cares? You're a bloody urban yogi!

"Sofa Savasana": Who says yoga has to be all fancy stretches and impossible poses? Grab your comfiest blanket, lie down on the sofa, and indulge in some Savasana. Bonus points if you've got a telly show playing in the background - multitasking at its finest!

"Kitchen Counter Karma": Turn your kitchen into a makeshift yoga studio. Use the kitchen counter for support as you stretch and bend, and feel the Zen vibes flow as you whip up a nice meal. Just watch out for flying vegetables if you get too carried away!

"Bedtime Bliss": Make bedtime a Zen affair by incorporating some gentle stretching and deep breathing before you hit the hay. It's the perfect way to unwind and prepare for a good night's kip, all without the need for any bug-infested nature spots.

"Bathroom Breathing Break": Take a moment of peace and quiet in the loo (don't worry, no one needs to know!). Close your eyes, take a few deep breaths, and let the stress of the day wash away. Just don't fall asleep in there - that might raise some eyebrows!

"Pavement Poses": Who needs a fancy yoga mat when you've got the pavement? Find a quiet spot on the side-walk, do some stretching and balancing poses, and show the world that you can find your Zen anywhere - even in the middle of a bustling city.

So here you have it, a bunch of hilarious and practical alternatives to "yoga in nature." Remember, the key to finding your Zen is to embrace the silliness, have a laugh, and most importantly, do what feels right for you. Whether you're a nature-loving yogi or a city-dwelling Zen master, the important thing is to keep exploring and enjoying the wonderful world of yoga in your own unique way.

NamasTea, you fabulous bunch of yogi adventurers! May your yoga journey continue to be filled with laughter, fun, and a healthy dose of bloody charm. Cheers to finding your Zen wherever the heck you fancy!

The Pub Pose

Why, you cheeky bugger, might you wonder why a pub's nestled in the wild and nature? 'Ave you ever graced a proper pub in the bloody UK? Let me tell ya, some of these establishments are like stepping into a parallel universe—a wild, uncensored realm teeming with the most peculiar species you'll ever set your bleary eyes on.

First up, we got the Pint-Sized Philosopher, often seen gazing into his beer like he's deciphering the mysteries of the universe—except his genius insights typically end up as a crumpled beer mat. And don't forget Ol' Slurry Steve, the bloke who's convinced he's practising "liquid yoga," seamlessly transitioning from the Lotus Pose to the Slouched Slurp. You'll spot him in the corner, attempting to balance his pint glass with the grace of a newborn giraffe on roller skates.

Oh, let's not ignore the Lager-ed Luminary, who's certain he's discovered the yogic secrets to eternal peace at the bottom of his tenth pint. Trust me, mate, his alignment might be wonkier than a bent cucumber, but he's convinced he's reached the spiritual realm of the almighty Ale-sana. And then there's the Prana Punk, decked out in tie-dye leggings, serenading the barmaid with drunken renditions of "Om" while clutching a bottle of organic kombucha. A real sight for sore eyes, that one.

Now, why am I blabbering on about these pub patrons? Well, dear BnB, this motley crew of inebriated oddballs is the perfect backdrop to our wild yoga tale. Just picture it: a dingy pub corner transformed into a makeshift yoga studio, where the Lager-ed Luminary tries to fold himself into a Lotus Pose without toppling over like a house of cards. Meanwhile, the Prana Punk attempts to lead the group in an impromptu chant of "Namaste, You Wankers!" And as for Ol' Slurry Steve, well, he's pretty much nailed the art of the Sloppy Savasana, sprawled out on a bar stool in blissful ignorance.

The "Pub Pose"

A bloody classic among the ale-loving yogis, innit? Picture this sh!te: you've had a proper rough day at work, and all you can think of is heading straight to the nearest pub for a pint of liquid gold. But wait, why the hell not combine your love for a good brew with a wee bit of mindfulness?

Enter the "Pub Pose"

A unique f@cking yoga position designed specifically for those who want to find their inner peace while still enjoying the delightful chaos of a busy pub. Here's how it goes, mate:

1. you stroll into the pub

2. making a beeline for the bar and with a pint in hand, you find a little corner to call your own.

3. As you take your first sip of that lovely ale, you close your eyes and take a deep breath - the f@cking quintessential beginning of any yoga practice. The loud chatter and clinking of glasses become your background music, and you let the ambiance of the pub wash over you.

4. Now, in this pose, f@cking balance is key. You have to find that sweet spot where you can enjoy your drink without spilling it all over yourself. The wobbles and sways are all part of the f@cking fun, of course - who the f@ck said yoga had to be all serious and rigid?

5. And let's not forget the f@cking mindfulness aspect of the "Pub Pose." As you savour each sip of that golden nectar, you let go of all the worries and stress from the day. You immerse yourself in the f@cking present moment, fully embracing the joy of the pub atmosphere.

But wait, there's more, mate! The "Pub Pose" also comes with its own set of variations. For those feeling particularly adventurous, you can try the "Beer Balance" - a daring move where you attempt to hold your pint glass on your head while maintaining your composure.

Now, I must warn you, mate - the "Pub Pose" is not without its f@cking challenges. You might encounter curious onlookers or even fellow yogi enthusiasts who want to join in on the fun. But fear not, for the "Pub Pose" is all about letting go of your inhibitions and embracing the sheer delight of being a bit daft.

The yoga in the wild, with a side of pub culture that'll leave you chuckling into your pint. 'Cause if you think the natural world's wild, you've clearly never experienced the uproarious chaos of a British boozer. Cheers to bendy poses and unsteady pints, and remember, in this chapter, even our yoga mats might have a slight ale aroma. Just roll with it, 'cause ain't no one doing the Downward Dog like these blokes and their pints!

So there you have it, the "Pub Pose" - a f@cking hilarious and unconventional way to find your Zen amidst the hustle and bustle of a lively pub. Cheers to raisin' your glass and finding your inner peace in the most unexpected places. NamasTea, my ale-loving yogi friends, and may your "Pub Pose" adventures be filled with laughter, good company, and a pint or two of your favourite brew!

Chapter 19

LOVERS

Let's delve into the twisted world of Tinder romance with these yoga fanatics, shall we? For the lads out there, swipe right on a yoga guru enthusiast, and ye might find yourself caught in a bizarre yoga fantasy-land. They'll be chatting you up with phrases like "namaste" and "finding inner peace," but don't be fooled – it's more like finding yourself tangled in a web of yoga jargon.

Picture this – you match with a yoga fanatic, and they're all keen to show off their "yoga skills" in the bedroom. They'll be suggesting all sorts of bendy positions, but let's face it, lads – they're more flexible with their words than their bodies. You'll be struggling to keep up with their "yoga-inspired" moves, and it's less like a passionate romp and more like a yoga class gone wrong.

For the lassies out there, swiping right on a yoga enthusiast is a whole other story. They'll be chatting you up with cheesy lines like "let's flow together" or "our chakras are aligning." It's like they've got a script straight out of a yoga-themed romcom. And let's not forget their obsession with matching their yoga mats with their yoga pants – it's like they're dressing for a f@cking yoga-themed fashion show!

But beware, lassies, because they'll be trying to convert ye to their yoga ways. They'll be inviting you to yoga classes like it's a bloody religious experience, and you'll find yourself surrounded by a sea of sweaty bodies twisting into pretzels. And let's not forget the awkward post-yoga coffee date, where they'll be raving about the "spiritual connection" they felt in class. It's like they've entered a whole other dimension of romantic weirdness.

And their social media game? They'll be posting pictures of themselves in all sorts of yoga poses – in the park, at the beach, even on top of a bloody mountain! It's like they're trying to prove that yoga is the answer to all of life's problems. But let's be real here – a handstand in front of the Eiffel Tower doesn't make you a guru.

The roller-coaster of romance with these yoga fanatics on Tinder. It's a wild ride of cheesy lines, bendy bedfellows, and awkward encounters. But hey, who said love was meant to be easy? Swipe right if ye dare, but be prepared for a yoga-infused adventure like no other. And remember, lads and lassies, keep a sense of humour handy – you'll need it in the crazy world of yoga romance!

Picture this: a match made in yogic heaven, two yoga guru enthusiasts locking eyes across the studio. Sparks fly as they twist and contort themselves into the most ridiculous yoga poses, like a pair of bendy acrobats in a circus act. They're all om-ing and ohm-ing, surrounded by a cloud of incense and mysticism.

But let's not be fooled, folks! This romance is far from the peaceful, Zen-filled fairy tale ye might imagine. No, no, it's more like a chaotic circus with some expletive-filled acrobatics thrown in for good measure.

They're on a date, right? But instead of enjoying a lovely dinner, they're doing yoga together in the park. Can you f@cking believe it? They're trying to one-up each other with the most outlandish poses, all in the name of romance. "Look at me, darling, I can balance on one finger while reciting a mantra!" And the other one's like, "Oh yeah? Well, watch me do a handstand on a tree branch!" It's like a battle of the yoga titans, but with a lot more sweating and cursing.

On their bedroom antics, if you can call it that. They're trying to get it on in all sorts of crazy yoga positions that not even the Kamasutra would dare to dream up. It's like watching a contortionist act in a circus tent, but with a lot more grunts and groans. And let's just say that some of these poses are not as sexy as they might think. Ye know what they say, folks – yoga is not always the key to unlocking the bedroom door.

But hey, they're in love, right? And love makes ye do some crazy things. So they keep bending and stretching themselves into all sorts of ridiculous shapes, thinking it's the path to eternal bliss. But little do they know that love and yoga don't always go hand in hand. Sometimes, it's best to keep the yoga on the mat and leave the romance to more conventional positions.

And as their love story unfolds, they find themselves in the midst of a social media whirlwind. Ye see, these yoga guru enthusiasts can't resist showing off their love and acrobatics to the world. Their Instagram feeds are filled with a never-ending stream of yoga-inspired couple photos, complete with cheesy captions like "Twisted in love" and "Bending our way through life together."

But let me tell ya, the world is not always as enamoured with their yogic romance as they are. Some people can't help but roll their eyes at the endless display of contorted limbs and spiritual mumbo-jumbo. "Oh, look at them, trying to be all deep and meaningful with their yoga love," they scoff. "It's just a bunch of circus tricks if you ask me."

And then there are the Tinder escapades. You'd think that being a yoga guru enthusiast would make it easier to find a match, right? But oh no, it's a whole other level of madness. They're swiping left and right like there's no tomorrow, looking for that perfect yogi soulmate. "Sorry, not flexible enough for me," they say, dismissing potential matches with a flick of their thumb.

But every now and then, they come across someone who's equally obsessed with all things yoga. And what happens next is a match made in downward dog heaven. They start trading yoga tips and tricks, discussing their favourite poses and the best yoga retreats in the world. It's like a secret yoga society, and they're the proud members, bound by their love for all things bendy and spiritual.

But even in this yoga-loving world, there are bound to be bumps in the road. They argue over who has the better alignment in their Warrior II, or who can hold a headstand for longer. And when they try to meditate together, it's like a battle of wills to see who can stay in silence the longest. It's like a yogic version of "who blinks first."

But despite all the ups and downs, they keep coming back to their mat, finding solace and comfort in each other's practice. And maybe, just maybe, their love for yoga will be the one thing that keeps their relationship grounded amidst all the chaos.

A romance filled with yoga, laughter, and a whole lot of swearing. It's a love story like no other, a circus of emotions and contortions that will leave ye scratching your heads and laughing your arses off. But hey, love is a journey, and sometimes, ye just gotta embrace the absurdity of it all. The yoga guru enthusiasts – the bendy, the spiritual, and the slightly insane. May they continue their quest for love and enlightenment, one yoga pose at a time. And may they never stop sharing their love and laughter with the world, even if it means embarrassing themselves in the process. Because in the end, love is a beautiful mess, and there's no better way to embrace it than with a good ol' laugh and a whole lot of yoga.

NamasTea, my friends, NamasTea.

Chapter 20

YOGA ENTHUSIAST AND THEIR WACKY JOBS

The Office Worker Turned Yogi Guru:

Picture this – the once stiff and stressed-out office worker who's now a yoga enthusiast. They've turned their cubicle into a mini yoga studio, and every morning, before tackling spreadsheets, they lead their colleagues through a mandatory Sun Salutation routine. From Warrior Pose to Tree Pose, they've got the whole office bending and stretching like a bunch of new-age warriors. The boss might not be thrilled, but hey, at least they've all got their chakras aligned before the morning coffee break.

The Dog Walker with a Zen Twist:

This yoga enthusiast has found a way to combine their love for dogs and yoga into a quirky job. As they stroll through the park with a pack of pooches, they seamlessly transition into yoga poses to keep the pups entertained. Watch in amazement as they do a perfect Downward Dog while surrounded by actual dogs. It's like a yoga class for canines, and let's face it, these dogs have never been calmer.

The Yoga-obsessed Barista:

Forget your regular coffee shop experience – this barista takes latte art to a whole new level. As they expertly craft your cappuccino, they're also demonstrating intricate yoga poses on the counter. With each swirl of frothy milk, they strike a Warrior Pose, and as they hand you your drink, they hold a perfect Tree Pose. Who knew coffee and yoga could be such a harmonious blend?

The Yoga Handyman: This handyman is not your average Joe with a toolbox. Oh no, they fix things with a twist – literally. As they repair your leaky faucet, they're busting out their yoga moves, doing a Headstand to reach those hard-to-reach spots. And don't be surprised if they end up in a Lotus Pose while fixing the wiring – it's all in a day's work for this yogi handyman.

The Yoga Teacher Turned Taxi Driver:

Say goodbye to boring taxi rides, 'cause this yoga enthusiast has turned their cab into a mobile yoga studio. As they navigate the city streets, they're also guiding their passengers through a series of soothing stretches and deep breaths. It's like a relaxing yoga class on wheels, complete with traffic jams and honking horns.

The Yoga-loving Waiter:

Ever been served a plate of food by someone who looks like they belong on a yoga mat instead of a restaurant floor? Well, meet the yoga-loving waiter who takes balancing trays to a whole new level. They effortlessly deliver your order while striking yoga poses that would put a contortionist to shame. Just don't be surprised if they take a quick Savasana break between courses.

The Yoga DJ:

This yoga enthusiast has combined their passion for music and yoga into a unique profession. As they spin tunes at the hottest nightclub in town, they're also guiding the crowd through impromptu yoga sessions. Watch as the partygoers bust out their best yoga moves on the dance floor – it's like a nightclub and yoga studio all rolled into one.

The Yoga-loving Bus Driver:

Forget the traditional bus ride – this bus driver has turned their double-decker into a yoga sanctuary on wheels. As they navigate the city streets, they're also leading passengers through a calming yoga flow. From Cat-Cow Pose to Cobra Pose, it's a yoga class with a view, as you watch the world go by from your window seat.

The Yoga Chef:

Who needs a regular chef when you can have a yoga enthusiast whip up your gourmet meal? As they chop vegetables and sauté onions, they're also demonstrating impressive yoga poses in the kitchen. It's like watching a culinary master and yoga guru all in one – a feast for the eyes and the taste buds.

The Yoga-loving Uber Driver:

This uber-cool uber driver takes your ride to a whole new level with their yoga expertise. As they navigate the city streets, they're also leading you through a mini yoga session. From seated stretches to breath-work, it's a Zen ride you won't forget. Just don't be surprised if they ask for a 5-star review – after all, who wouldn't rate a yoga ride with top marks?

The Yoga-Posing UPS Driver:

Who needs a typical UPS delivery when you can have a yoga enthusiast show up at your door? This driver has turned package delivery into a yoga extravaganza. Picture them gracefully lunging forward to place your parcel on the doorstep, or maybe even doing a swift Warrior III as they hand you your package. It's like a yoga performance with each delivery, leaving customers both impressed and slightly bewildered.

The Zen Hairdresser:

This hairdresser has taken their passion for yoga to the salon chair. As they expertly snip and style your hair, they're also contorting themselves into yoga poses that would put a Russian dancer with arthritis to shame. It's a hairdressing session and yoga class all rolled into one, leaving you with a fabulous haircut and a newfound appreciation for the art of balance.

The Yogi Doctor:

Say hello to the doctor who practices medicine with a side of yoga. As they diagnose and treat patients, they're also sneaking in a few yoga stretches and breathing exercises. Picture them doing a gentle seated twist while listening to your heartbeat, or maybe even a calming Child's Pose during your check-up. It's a whole new approach to healthcare, and you can't help but feel a little more relaxed in their care.

The Yoga-Loving Police Officer:

This police officer knows how to keep the peace and strike a pose. Picture them confidently directing traffic with a Warrior Pose, or maybe even doing a calming Tree Pose during a tense situation. It's like having your very own yoga guru keeping the city safe, one pose at a time.

The Yoga Flight Attendant:

Who needs in-flight entertainment when you can have a yoga enthusiast as your flight attendant? Picture them leading passengers through a series of calming stretches and breathing exercises during the flight. From seated twists to airplane-friendly Downward Dogs, it's a yoga class at 30,000 feet, leaving travellers feeling both relaxed and entertained.

The Yogi Chef:

This chef has elevated cooking to a whole new level with their yoga expertise. As they chop, sauté, and season, they're also effortlessly flowing through yoga poses in the kitchen. Picture them doing a graceful Warrior II as they stir the pot or maybe even a balancing Half Moon Pose while plating your meal. It's a culinary masterpiece and a yoga performance all in one.

The Yoga-loving Firefighter:

When they're not putting out fires, this firefighter is striking yoga poses to stay centred and focused. Picture them doing a powerful Warrior I before charging into a burning building or a grounding Mountain Pose during a moment of reflection. It's a firefighter with a Zen twist, keeping the community safe and serene.

The Yoga Librarian:

This librarian has found a way to incorporate yoga into their love for books and knowledge. Picture them doing a seated forward fold between bookshelves or a gentle Cat-Cow Pose during story-time for children. It's a library experience that's both enlightening and educational, leaving library-goers with a newfound appreciation for the art of relaxation.

The Yoga Detective:

This detective has a unique approach to solving crimes – with a little help from yoga. Picture them doing a calming breathing exercise to clear their mind during an investigation or a fierce Warrior III as they chase down a suspect. It's a detective on the case and on the mat, solving mysteries with a touch of tranquillity.

So there you have it – a glimpse into the world of yoga enthusiasts and their unconventional jobs. From package delivery to hairdressing, from medicine to law enforcement, these yogis are bringing their passion for yoga into every aspect of their lives. It's a blend of humour, balance, and a whole lot of flexibility, leaving us all with a smile and a newfound appreciation for the art of yoga.

NamasTea, fellow workers!

Ciao Ciao the Yogrand Finale

Well, ain't this a bloody moment? We've reached the grand finale of our utterly daft exploration of yoga without all that bloody spirituality malarkey. Let's take a f@cking moment to ponder the unconventional path we've slogged through and the bloody brilliant benefits we've snagged from this alternative approach to yoga (well I was more taking a piss of it really!).

Let's give a right good toss to the elephant in the yoga studio—the spiritual bollocks of this ancient practice. Some of us ain't too keen on diving into the depths of our souls or pondering the cosmic sh!te while we're struggling to contort ourselves like a bunch of clowns. And you know what? That's fine and dandy, mates! This book's for all you lot who prefer your yoga with a generous side of snark, a pinch of scepticism, and a wanker's dose of eye-rolling.

Spirituality? Piss right off with that nonsense! We've got enough baffling existential questions to make our heads spin, and we're supposed to add more? Bugger that! With taxes to pay, appointments to keep, and a never-ending list of responsibilities, yoga should be our f@cking escape, a sanctuary from the mundane crap, a chance to unleash our inner bloody goof-ball.

Throughout this topsy-turvy yogic journey, we've discovered that laughter is the ultimate antidote to all that bleeding seriousness. As we've attempted those daft poses and renamed the classics with downright bonkers monikers, we've found solace in the fact that life doesn't have to be a bloody lecture in existential wankery. Sometimes, it's perfectly alright to roll out the mat, strike a pose, and let out a hearty guffaw at the sheer absurdity of it all.

Meditation? Bah, who needs it! While some folks may find peace in the silence, the rest of us end up with a head full of distractions. So, why not embrace the chaos, you bunch of cheeky BnB? Instead of sitting cross-legged trying to empty your head, imagine yourself as a superhero zooming through the sky, dodging obstacles, and saving the world from all that mundane bollocks.

And don't you dare forget the physical benefits! While we've been taking the mickey out of the spiritual side, we've also been stretching and flexing our bodies, balancing like drunken sailors, and discovering muscles we never knew existed. Why bother with them ancient Sanskrit-named poses when you can achieve the same f@cking results by flailing your limbs and calling it the "Tangled Pretzel Pose"?

Oh, and stress relief? No need for them serene chants and calming mantras. We've got something even better—a good, hearty belly laugh! So, go ahead and giggle your arse off, you lot! Let the tears of joy stream down your face as you attempt the yoga positions with a twist. Trust me, you'll feel lighter, happier, and definitely less inclined to take life too f@cking seriously.

Spirituality ain't for everyone, and that's just fine by us. You can achieve peace, physical flexibility, and a well-deserved chuckle without having to buy into any bloody belief system.

Remember, this journey is yours to make your bloody own. Roll up your mat, tie it into a pretzel, or use it as a makeshift superhero cape. Embrace the unconventional, dare to be different, and never forget to find joy in the simple act of laughter.

Life is too short to be serious all the bloody time

So, bugger off, my fellow unconventional yogis, and may your path be paved with laughter, flexibility, and a healthy dose of sarcasm.

THANK YOU SO MUCH and hopefully you had fun reading this as I wrote it.

NamasF@ckingTea Everyone!

Note from the Author:

Hey there, Amazing Readers,

As you've gone on this wild ride with me through the funny world of yoga, I just want to say a big thanks for coming along. I need to remind you that this book was never meant to make fun of yoga or the folks who love it. Yoga is a special thing for many, bringing them peace and good vibes.

The point of this book was to make you laugh and see the funny side of yoga, especially the parts that aren't super serious. It's supposed to be a fun read with lots of jokes.

I really believe that humour can make life better, and that's why I wanted to make yoga funny. But remember, this book isn't a definite guide to yoga, and it doesn't mean yoga isn't meaningful to lots of people.

So, as we look back on this funny journey, I hope you remember all the times we laughed together, and I hope you had fun seeing yoga from a goofy angle. And did you like the "Winasana" and "Yogavocado" poses? I sure hope so. And by the way, I drew all the pictures myself, covers included.

Thanks a million for choosing to take this funny adventure with me. I hope it put a smile on your face, made you giggle, and reminded you that life can be a bit crazy but also pretty awesome.

With lots of thanks,

*A.S.Salomone

*You lovely rascals, Antonio "Salo" Salomone! Salo is my nickname since the secondary school… and Of course, it was all part of the plan to have the word "**ASS**" boldly displayed on the book's cover! ;-)

Printed in Great Britain
by Amazon

38533835R00106